PERSONAL COMP
COMPUTER ILLITERATE

MW01275269

THE WHAT, WHEN, WHERE, HOW, AND WHY
GUIDE TO UNDERSTANDING, BUYING,
AND USING

PERSONAL COMPUTERS FOR THE COMPUTER ILLITERATE

BARRY OWEN

HarperPerennial
A Division of HarperCollinsPublishers

Grateful acknowledgement is made to the following for permission to reprint the following copyrighted material:

Anne Sexton: "The Earth" (excerpt) from *The Awful Rowing Toward God* by Anne Sexton. Copyright © 1975 by Loring Conant, Jr., Executor of the Estate of Anne Sexton. Reprinted by permission of Houghton Mifflin Company.

Eugene Ehrlich: Excerpt from *Amo, Amas, Amat and More.* Copyright © 1985 by Eugene Ehrlich. Reprinted by permission of HarperCollins Publishers, Inc.

FIRST EDITION

Designed by Joan Greenfield
Illustrations by Ed Taber

Library of Congress Cataloging-in-Publication Data

Owen, Barry, 1952–
   Personal computers for the computer illiterate/by Barry Owen.—1st ed.
      p.   cm.
   Includes index.
   ISBN 0-06-096839-7 (pbk.)
   1. Microcomputers.   I. Title.
QA76.5.O96   1990
004.16—dc20   90-55005

---

91 92 93 94 95 DT/HC 10 9 8 7 6 5 4 3 2 1

For my father, Major C. T. Owen, USAF (Ret.)

CONTENTS

ACKNOWLEDGEMENTS

In writing this book, I feel closer to my intended readers, computer illiterates, than to the wizards and experts who readily and generously shared their knowledge with me. I am especially grateful, then, that the wizards and experts I know have shared their knowledge so readily and generously, for I could not have written this book without them. I'm thinking especially of Paul Somerson, Editorial Director of *PC Sources*; Bill Machrone, Editor-in-Chief of *PC Magazine*; Gus Venditto, Executive Editor of *PC Magazine*; Ellen Atkinson, Director of Marketing, *PC Magazine*; Luisa Simone, independent consultant; Connie Winkler, also an independent consultant; John Dickinson, Editor of *PC Computing*; Fred Davis, *PC Week* Lab Director (and former editor of *MacUser*); Nancy Groth, Managing Editor of *MacUser*; Michael Frayn, editor and writer; Rich Landry, Editor-in-Chief of *PC World*; and Karl Koessel, Technical Editor of *PC World*. Thanks also to Queen Posy of Terranamae for pertinent, perspicacious commentary from beginning to end; James Langdell for giving the manuscript a technical read; Dianne Platner for recommending Ed Taber to me; Ed Taber for his delightful illustrations; my editor, Rick Kot, for his forbearance (and for dinner thrice); and to Rick's understanding, always helpful and encouraging assistant, Sheila Gillooly.

I am especially grateful to the dozens of people I met while working on this book, who, when I described it to them, immediately declared, "That's for me!" Finally, thank you, Eric, for making me do this and seeing it through to the end—and to the beginning. H^2.

INTRODUCTION: WHO NEEDS THIS BOOK AND HOW TO USE IT

The What, When, Where, How, and Why Guide to Understanding, Buying, and Using Personal Computers for the Computer Illiterate is for you if . . .

1   You're thinking of buying a personal computer and definitely want to buy smart—but don't know where to begin.

2   You already own or use a PC, but have a funny feeling that your machine could do a lot more for you. You want to know more about hardware and software options and opportunities, including how to choose and where to buy printers, applications, accessories, and so forth, and where to find technical help.

3   You own a PC and are reasonably comfortable with it, but want a better understanding—if not a complete technical education—in how the system works.

4   You don't own or use a PC and you're not planning to buy one—not just yet anyway—but you'd like to know what the heck all the commotion's about.

If you identify with any of the needs described above, you'll find answers and advice you can use in the pages that follow.

There are two ways to use *The WWWH&W Guide:* by reading straight through from beginning to end, or by reading selectively.

1

If you're a self-proclaimed "complete idiot"—a noble, striving self-proclaimed complete idiot—when it comes to personal computers, you would do best to begin at the beginning (Section 1: "What Is a Personal Computer?") and read straight through.

If you're already familiar with basic terms and concepts of personal computing but need help deciding what PC to buy, start with Section 5, "How to Choose a Personal Computer." This explains how to select a personal computer that suits your current and future needs. It also describes the system options available, including IBM PC compatible, IBM PS/2, Apple II, Apple Macintosh, Atari, and Next desktop and laptop machines.

If you currently own or use a PC and want to know more about what you can do with it, how it works, where to get help, or other information, turn to the appropriate section listed in the table of contents.

At the end of *The WWWH&W Guide* you'll find a section entitled "Antidotes to PC Illiteracy," which is part glossary and part index. Look here first when searching for particular PC-related definitions and explanations. This section also includes facts, terms, phrases, and background that veteran PC users and PC professionals—including salespeople—often use to impress, intimidate, and sometimes even to illuminate the rest of us.

A note about the order of this book: Most general guides to personal computers—not that there are very many to choose from—written for aspiring or new users discuss hardware first and applications software second. Virtually all veteran users and outright authorities on the subject, however, advise beginners to "start with software." In other words, decide what you want to do with a personal computer—choose your initial applications—before selecting a PC or shopping for hardware components like video display terminals or printers to attach to it. *Personal Computers for the Computer Illiterate: The What, When, Where, How, and Why Guide* accepts, endorses, and practices this good, nearly universal advice. That's why the section on applications comes before the section on hardware.

1

WHAT IS
A PERSONAL
COMPUTER?

ABOUT THIS SECTION

Most computer books botch it when it comes to explaining what a personal computer is . . . unless you've used one long enough to already know from experience what a PC is.

Many computer science teachers can explain what personal computers are, all right, as long as you're a future computer scientist yourself.

As for veteran personal computer users: They try (and we're grateful for their efforts), but too often they're about as illuminating as a candle in a hailstorm.

The typical textbook explanation of what a PC is runs something like this: A personal computer is a device equipped to receive data in a prescribed form, process the data, and generate results in a specified format as information or as highly organized electrical pulses used to control other machines or related processes.

But what in the vast cosmos does this mean? Since I'm not sure, I've prepared a somewhat different explanation of a personal computer. That's what this section is about.

A personal computer—or PC as it's usually called—is not just one machine; it's a collection of plastic and metal that can be turned into many different kinds of specialized machines. A single PC, for example, can be turned into

- a machine that makes preaddressed mailing labels
- a machine that helps you learn French or Spanish or Russian or helps you prepare for the SAT or teaches preschoolers letter, number, and color recognition
- a machine that stores and automatically sorts through huge quantities of information, the kind of information traditionally kept on paper in manila folders and file cabinets
- a machine that designs and produces everything from homemade greeting cards and church newsletters to slick advertisements and glossy magazines
- a machine that makes fast, complex business projections or keeps tax records or analyzes investment opportunities
- an electronic arcade-style pinball machine
- a machine that sends messages to and receives written messages from other PCs via telephone lines anywhere in the world
- a machine that keeps track of all the sales, expenses, client or patient records, and other details of a retail or service-oriented business or a professional practice
- an incredibly fast, versatile writing and text editing machine that makes typing seem like etching in stone

This is the short list of PC specialties. You'll find the long list in Section 3, "Applications and Activities: Get with the Program," starting on page 21.

The fact that you can transform a PC into dozens of different specialized machines sets it apart from just about every other kind of device for the home or office you can think of—with the possible exception of a fancy food processor.

Consider the CD player, for example. It does one thing: plays compact disks.

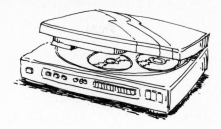

A washing machine does one thing: It cleans dirty laundry.

A camera does one thing: It takes pictures.

A car does one thing: It transports you from one place to another.

All of these machines are dedicated to a single purpose. In computer lingo they're called *dedicated machines*.

Personal computers are *not* dedicated machines; they

are inert, more-or-less mindless boxes that have the potential to become many different kinds of machines.

To be more precise, *a personal computer is whatever you turn it into.*

The key word in the preceding sentence is "you."

For unlike the big computers, called *mainframes*, the kind used to guide interplanetary space probes and predict global weather patterns and keep track of 50 zillion tax returns, personal computers are designed primarily for people like you and me, people who are not computer specialists. They're designed to be used by individuals; that's why they're called *personal.*

PCs may be designed for people who aren't computer specialists, but they can't read your mind. You can't walk up to a PC and say, "Hmmm, I think I'd like to learn a little French this afternoon, *s'il vous plaît*," and expect it to suddenly turn itself into an electronic French tutor.

If you want to turn your PC into an electronic French tutor for the afternoon, you've got to convert it into one using *application software*, or application *programs*, as they're often called. Without application software, PCs are all but useless.

This is a key concept, worth repeating and elaborating. Personal computers, those dull, usually beige boxes with a TV sitting on top of them and a typewriter-like keyboard in front of them are good for just about nothing in and of themselves. If you want to use a PC to write a report or design a newsletter or create a spreadsheet or to file data or any of a thousand other things, you need application software. You use this software to convert idle, mindless PCs to specialized machines for work, study, and play.

The beginning of this section posed a question: "What is a PC?" Now you know the answer: A PC is many different machines. You convert it from one kind of machine to another by using application software. As far as most PC users are concerned, application software is the entire point of having a personal computer.

What does application software look like? How do you use it to convert a PC into a specialized machine? Once you've made the conversion, what do you do next? For answers to these timely questions, and a few others, proceed to Section 2, "Working with the System."

2

WORKING
WITH
THE SYSTEM

Even if you're on the right track, you'll get run over if you just sit there. —WILL ROGERS

ABOUT THIS SECTION

A camera is good for one thing: taking pictures. A car is also good for one thing. Ditto a calculator, a copier, and most other contemporary contraptions. The fact is, just about every machine or device you can think of is dedicated to a single rigid function.

But not personal computers. PCs are far-ranging free spirits. They're protean, capable of being converted to dozens of different kinds of specialized machines. That's why they're attractive to so many different types of people and businesses.

But the transformation of a PC from an inert hunk of metal and plastic to a specialized machine doesn't occur spontaneously, as if by magic. You, the user, have to make it happen.

You don't, however, have to be a conjurer, witch doctor, or computer scientist to convert a PC to a specialized machine—or to become a skilled PC user. What you do need is application software. You also need to become familiar with the parts of a personal computer, what they do, and how to make them work for you. That's what this section is about: naming the parts of a PC system, describing what they do and how to use them. Please read on.

TWO KINGDOMS: SOFTWARE AND HARDWARE

Here's what a typical personal computer system looks like.

The Macintosh® IIx personal computer. (Photo courtesy of Apple Computer, Inc.)

More accurately, here's what the typical *hardware* parts of a PC system look like. These parts are called hardware for the most practical, straightforward, and uncorrupted of reasons: because they're tactile . . . tangible . . . sporting surfaces and edges. . . . They have substance and weight. . . . You can touch them and feel them, hold them and carry them. In short, hardware's called hardware because it's hard.

But personal computers are more than the picture-hogging hardware shown above. PCs are also software: electronic instructions and information that, like recorded music, can be created, stored, and manipulated, but cannot be touched or held, at least not in the same obvious way as hardware.

Software may be intangible, but it is every bit as important as hardware, for without software, all that gleaming high-tech metal and plastic in the picture is good for nothing. On the other hand, the only way to get at the software, to create it and store it and manipulate it, is with hardware.

FOCUS ON SOFTWARE

A fundamental truth—*the* fundamental truth—about personal computers bears repeating (even though you just read it): For all its solid virtues, a personal computer is useless on its own; it's a severed head, a brain without a mind, good for nothing. *Nada. Pfft!* The PC is useless, that is, without software. A personal computer's mind, its can-do, get-up-and-go, got-what-it-takes intelligence, its multiple personalities, its ability to specialize—in short, its raison d'être—reside not in the obvious, straightforward, solid-as-a-breadbox hardware (although hardware is essential, of course), but in the intangible, solid-as-the-wind software.

Lots of bright people have trouble understanding this, mainly, I think, because software is so literally . . . ungraspable. The good news: You don't have to understand how software works in order to use it, or even to master it. If such understanding were required, you can be sure that 90 percent of all PC users—nay, 98 percent, including, for the longest time, this writer—would be reduced to using their PCs as conversation items and doorstops. So don't worry about how software works. The trick is to understand how to use it.

There are several different kinds of software, but as a user, you only need to know about three kinds: applications, system software, and data. A fourth category of software, machine or "hidden" software, is placed permanently inside every personal computer at the time it's manufactured. Hidden software is explained below.

APPLICATIONS You already know what applications (apps) are; they're the kind of software that converts PCs from good-for-nothing hunks of dull beige metal and plastic to specialized machines that create newsletters, file reports, teach French, and so forth. And specialized machines, you'll recall, are what PCs are all about.

SYSTEM SOFTWARE *System software* is the master program that controls PC hardware and applications, among other things. If application software is the star of the PC show, system software is the producer, director, and stage manager rolled into one. System software is sometimes called *operating system* (abbreviated *OS*; pronounce the letters: oh-ess).

System software is, in other words, as vital as blood. You have to activate the system software before you can use an application to convert your PC into a specialized machine. Many PCs are set up so that this happens automatically when you turn them on. Whether it's automatic or requires the participation of the user, activating the system software is called *booting up* the system.

Once you're up to speed on a personal computer, you may find yourself routinely using a half-dozen or more applications. But just one system software program will serve all your applications, whether you use 6 apps or 66.

DATA Data is simply the stuff—reports, statistics, electronic spreadsheets, music, pictures, and so forth—you create using applications. If you convert your PC to a specialized writing/text-editing machine (a word processor), for example, and use this application to compose a memo to your boss, that memo is data. If you use a graphics program to create bar charts, the bar charts are data. Anything you create with applications is data. To put it another way, applications are the kind of software you use to do work; data is the work you create using applications.

HIDDEN SOFTWARE There are other kinds of vital software, but they're hidden deep inside the central processing unit. You can't get at them, you can't alter them, you can't manipulate them (as you can manipulate system software, applications, and data). They're like the brain stem in human beings, responsible for controlling involuntary processes (breathing and digesting and the pumping of the heart). They're vital, in other words, but they function on a level that's beneath consciousness.

So don't worry about the computer's deep-brain software; the three kinds of software to know about are applications and system software and data.

USING APPLICATIONS Okay, so you need application software to convert a PC to a word processor, foreign language tutor, electronic game, or any of dozens of other kinds of specialized machines. But what do applications look like? How do you use them?

Like all software, applications are intangible; you

can't touch them or hold them. You can't see the pulses of electricity—the electronic instructions and information—that are the essence of software. This would seem to present an insurmountable problem. How can you use something you can't hold in your hands or size up with your own two eyes?

Well, whether you realize it or not, you do precisely this all the time. You can't hold household current in your hands, for example, but this doesn't stop you from harnessing it, controlling it, directing it, managing it . . . in short, using it.

The secret of harnessing household current is no secret at all: Since you can't use electricity directly you have to use it indirectly, by getting your hands on devices and machines that can use it directly.

Another example: You can't hold recorded music in your hands.

Yes, I know: You can hold cassette tapes in your hands. You can hold CDs in your hand. But tapes and CDs are merely containers, *media* to use the technical word, for storing the music. They're not the music itself. The music itself is nothing more than ungraspable, unseeable electrical impulses stored magnetically on the tape or digitally on the CD.

Music stored on cassette tape is software. Cassette tape recorders are hardware, the kind of hardware that changes the stored music to vibrations in the air, vibrations we can hear.

Applications and personal computers have a similar relationship. Applications are software. You can't hold the application in your hand, but you can hold the container, the medium, that the application is stored on. And you can use hardware, a personal computer, to *read* the medium, changing its contents to something you can see, manipulate, and use.

FLOPPY DISKS The most common media for storing music these days are cassettes and compact disks. The equivalent medium for PC software is called a *floppy disk*, or sometimes, a *diskette*. Once they've been around them for a while, most people just call them *floppies*, as in "Hand me that floppy over there, wudja?"

Floppies are used for storing system software, applications, and data.

All off-the-shelf applications are sold on floppy disks. The floppies come in a box accompanied by *documentation*, instructions on how to use the applications software.

To reiterate, floppies are to the PC what cassette tapes are to a tape player. Just as tape players have a mechanism for inserting cassettes, PCs have mechanisms for playing floppy disks . . . which brings us to hardware.

HARDWARE

Here's the same picture of a typical personal computer you saw at the beginning of this section, only this time with labels.

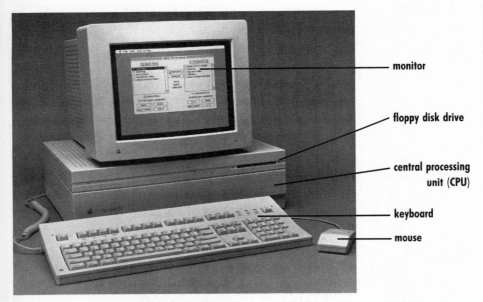

(Photo courtesy of Apple Computer, Inc.)

These components are the vital hardware organs of a personal computer. In PC lingo, they're called *system hardware*. Other hardware components, like printers, may be important, even essential to many kinds of work, but they are not critical in the same vital-organ, life-or-death sense. Printers and other nonvital components are called *peripheral hardware,* or just *peripherals*.

CENTRAL PROCESSING UNIT The PC's *central processing unit (CPU)* is its brain. Without software the CPU is a brain all right, but it's mindless, a brain without a clue—utterly dysfunctional and 100 percent useless.

The part of the CPU that you can see is mostly just a box. The real stuff, the working parts, are inside the box ("inside the box" is a favorite phrase of veteran PC users, especially the "wires-and-pliers" types). What's inside the box—the rest of the system hardware, and peripheral hardware are described in further detail in "Harnessing Hardware: Get a Grip," starting on page 76.

FLOPPY DISK DRIVES You introduce applications software, as well as system software and data, to the CPU from the outside. That's what those slots on the front of the box (the CPU) are for. They're called *floppy disk drives*. Not by coincidence, the *floppy drives*, as they're usually referred to, are just big enough to accommodate floppy disks, the medium used to store applications.

So it's really pretty simple. To convert a PC to an active specialized machine you insert the floppy disk containing the application (the software that converts the PC to a specialized machine) into the floppy drive. This is a strikingly similar scheme to cassette tape (software) and cassette tape recorders (hardware).

THE MONITOR After you've inserted the application (the floppy disk containing the application) into the floppy drive and converted the PC to a specialized machine, you need a way to see the application. If you can't see it, you can't work with it. Displaying the application is the job of the *monitor,* the part of the system that looks like a TV.

What you see on the monitor is a video worksheet. Video worksheets look different for every application.

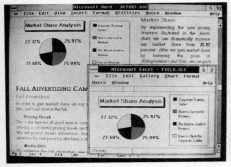 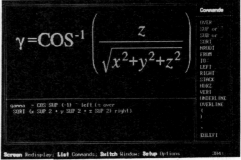

All personal computer applications display video worksheets or the equivalent on the monitor, the part of the system that looks like a TV screen. The worksheets are not static; you may use the keyboard or other devices to enter data—text, numbers, and graphics, for example—into the video worksheet and to alter the data, boldface a line of type, or perform a calculation. The applications shown are for Microsoft Word (*left,* courtesy of Microsoft Corporation) **and WordPerfect** (*right,* courtesy of WordPerfect Corporation), **both word processors.**

INPUT DEVICES You need something else before you can sit down at your system, convert it to a specialized machine, and start working. You need a way to control the whole shebang—to give it instructions, more commonly known as *commands,* and to *enter* data (write a letter, for example). The tools for doing these things are called *input devices.*

The most common input device is the *PC keyboard,* which looks a lot like an ordinary typewriter keyboard except for two differences: It has more keys, and instead of being built into the rest of the system, it's semidetached, connected by a cable. This gives you the freedom to move the keyboard around and even place it on your lap while working if you choose.

You don't need to know how to type to use a PC, by the way. Of course, typing skills give you an advantage for the same reason they give you an advantage on a conventional typewriter: You can locate keys faster. But an advantage is not the same as a necessity.

In the last few years, an input device called a *mouse* has also become popular, and for some applications, essential. While the computer mouse may not look anything like a keyboard, the similarities between the two are much greater than the differences. They're both used to do the same thing: give instructions—input commands—to the computer. By inputting commands you manipulate applications, work programs. You can also use a keyboard or mouse to create data, write a letter, or make a drawing, for example.

Computer keyboards work like regular typewriter keyboards, except that they come with specialized keys in addition to the familiar set of letter and number keys. You press keys or combinations of keys to control the machine. You use a computer mouse to do the very same thing, only in a different way. The mouse, in other words, like the keyboard, is an input device.

If you've never seen what an application looks like on the monitor, the part of the PC system that looks like a television, you'll have a very difficult time understanding how you can manipulate the application using a keyboard or mouse. If this is your case, I strongly advise you to get a demo from a friend or colleague or from a hardware or software store. Trying to understand how to manipulate an application from text is like trying to learn how to tie a shoe from written instructions. Seeing is understanding.

Most applications display commands on the screen of the monitor. These are either words ("Print," "Erase," "Calculate") or little pictures called icons that represent the words. Applications also display a little flashing pointer, called a cursor, on the screen. You manipulate applications, make them do what you want them to do, by moving the cursor from one command to another on the screen. You do this by tapping special arrow or cursor keys on the keyboard (left, right, up, down) or by grasping the mouse and moving it with your hand on a flat surface. The mouse's movement is mimicked on the screen by the cursor.

Older applications display what's called a command line, usually at the top of the screen. To manipulate such applications, you position the cursor on the line and type in the command. So-called "command-line applications" are rapidly becoming obsolete.

These days more and more PC users, newcomers and veterans, are opting to get both a keyboard and a mouse. The keyboard is essential because you need it to type words and numbers (create data). The mouse, however, is a much better tool for drawing lines and, in the experience of many users, for executing commands because all you have to do is point to a command and click the "Execute" button on the mouse. You can do this with one hand. It's so natural and intuitive that even beginners quickly become adept at "point-and-click" computing.

The keyboard and mouse are the principal input devices available to PC users. Alternatives are available, but they are ordinarily reserved for special purposes. You'll find a description of alternative input devices on pages 89–91.

HARD DISKS There's one other component of system hardware you need to learn about. It's not shown in the picture because it's more often hidden inside the central processing unit. It's called a *hard disk drive*, but most people shorten this to *hard disk, hard drive,* or *fixed disk*.

Hard disks are like floppy disks in that you can store software on them more or less permanently. Any kind of software that can be stored on floppy disks—system software, applications, and data—may also be stored on a hard disk. Their chief advantage: They can store many times the amount of software that can be stored on a single floppy. Another advantage: Applications generally work faster when stored on a hard disk.

These days most PC users have floppy disk drives and a hard disk. They keep all their software—system software, applications, and data—on the hard disk. This is more convenient because it eliminates the need to insert floppy disks into the floppy drives every time you want to start up the PC, convert it to a specialized machine, or retrieve data. With a hard disk, all your software can remain in one place, ready to use immediately, whenever you need it.

Strictly speaking, hard disks are not one of the PC's "vital organs"; you don't have to have one in order for your PC to function. But hard disks are so handy that few users opt to get along without one.

Okay pilgrims, if you think about it, you're really zipping along. You now know that PCs consist of both hardware and software. You further know the three key species of software are:

- system software (also called the operating system)
- applications (used to convert PCs to specialized machines)
- data (work created by using applications)

The PC's vital hardware organs are collectively known as system hardware. They include:

- central processing unit (CPU)
- input devices (usually a keyboard, a mouse, or both)
- monitor (looks like a TV)
- long-term memory units (hard and floppy disks and disk drives)

Software is stored more or less permanently in long-term memory, which is to say, on either or both floppy disks and the hard disk. These days most people keep much or all of their software (all kinds: system software, applications, and data) on a hard disk because this makes for more convenient storage and faster handling.

To use a PC you give it instructions (commands) using the keyboard or a computer mouse. These input devices are also used to create data (writing and drawing, for example). You view applications on the monitor.

When you pause to review what you know about PCs, its quite a lot, fellow strivers. In sum, you know the names of the key parts of a PC system. And you know, at least roughly, what they do.

The key to converting a personal computer to a specialized machine—a word processor or an electronic French teacher or even a computer game —is applications software. All applications software is sold on floppy disks (1).

As a user, your object is to make a copy of the software instructions from the floppy to the PC's electronic workspace, which is called RAM, short for random access memory. RAM is actually a collection of computer chips, spiderlike rectangles attached to the PC's motherboard, which is inside the central processing unit, usually referred to by its initials, CPU (2). To transfer the application from a floppy to RAM you have to insert the floppy into the floppy drive (3). Next you have to instruct the PC that you want it to make a copy of the application and place it in RAM. Such instructions are called "commands." You give the application commands by tapping designated keys on the keyboard (4), or by pointing and clicking a computer mouse (5). This command also instructs the PC to display the application on the monitor (6). In practice, this sequence of events usually doesn't take more than a few seconds.

After you've converted the inert PC to a specialized machine, you use the keyboard and/or a mouse to manipulate the application and to create work, which is usually called "data" among PC users. You can create all kinds of data with PCs, from text to spreadsheets to illustrations. Every application comes with its own array of commands for creating and altering data. You can also use commands to store your data on a floppy disk, print it on a printer (7), and transfer it via modem (8) and telephone lines to another PC across town or across the country.

These days, most people buy PCs containing a hard disk. Hard disks are like floppy disks except that they're usually not portable; you can't carry them around in your briefcase or purse. In fact, most hard disks are hidden inside the CPU. They're popular because they can hold a good deal more applications and data than floppy disks and because they minimize the need to swap floppy disks in and out of the floppy disk drive. Such "disk flopping" can easily become an annoyance if you routinely use more than one application or if you store your work—your data—on multiple floppies. Fortunately, it's easy to copy software from floppies to the hard disk, where it remains in permanent storage until you need it.

6

2

3

8

4

1

5

7

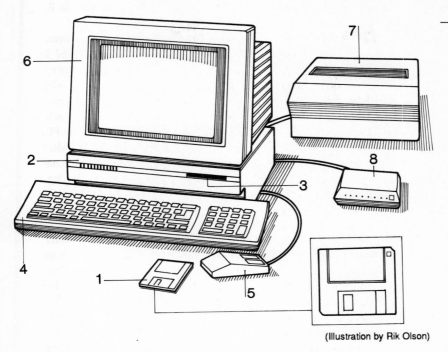

(Illustration by Rik Olson)

3

APPLICATIONS AND ACTIVITIES: GET WITH THE PROGRAM

E Unum Pluribus (Out of One, Many) —MOTTO OF THE UNITED STATES, REARRANGED

ABOUT THIS SECTION

Application is as dreary, workmanlike—as bureaucratic —a word as you can imagine . . . zzzz. But to experienced PC users, the dull, prosaic term *application* conjures up not the heavy-lidded sandman but . . . possibilities. Dozens, even hundreds of possibilities—or, to use a phrase favored by this book, specialized machines.

This section is all about specialized machines—that is, applications. Big apps and small ones. Applications popular and obscure. Serious apps and diverting apps. Applications for home, office, home office, small business, big business, inbetween-size business, classroom, nonprofit organization, government agency, professional practice, rugged individualist.

"Applications and Activities: Get with the Program" is divided into two parts. "The Choices" is about application categories (to list the name of every application available would require twenty volumes the size of this book). "The Rest of the Applications Story" clues you in to other important aspects of using applications you should be aware of before you set out to build your own applications library.

THE CHOICES

APPLICATIONS
AND
ACTIVITIES:
GET WITH
THE
PROGRAM

21

WORD PROCESSORS

If there's a single universal personal computer application, word processing is it. Virtually everyone who uses a
PC also uses a word processor. Many people buy personal
computers exclusively to take advantage of this one application, at least initially.

Word processing programs convert PCs into writing
and editing (revising) machines, but it's incorrect to
think of the word processor as simply an updated version
of the typewriter. There's at least an order-of-magnitude
($\times$ 10) difference between one and the other.

Think of it this way: Word processors are to typewriters what typewriters are to lead pencils with erasers
(and what pencils with erasers are to chisel and stone).

THE TYRANNY OF PAPER The difference between typewriters
and word processors starts with paper. Working with a
typewriter, of course, you must have paper. Word processors eliminate paper—at least while you're writing.
Instead of appearing on paper, your words appear on
the screen (the monitor).

To make the words appear on the screen, you type
on the PC keyboard just as you would on a regular
typewriter keyboard. Since the lines you're typing go
"to the screen," you don't have to add new sheets of
paper every time you come to the end of a page. Instead, the screen serves as an infinite electronic page,
somewhat like the cotton towel rollers found in some
public bathrooms.

When you complete a line on the screen, the word
processor starts a new line automatically, eliminating
the need to hit the Return key. This automatic word
wrapping allows you to type without interruption,
whether your document is two paragraphs long or two
hundred pages long. When you fill the screen up with
text, the top lines of the text automatically *scroll* out
of view, forming new space at the bottom. You can
"page up" or "page down" at any point to see text
that has scrolled out of view.

At any time, you may print your document on
paper, assuming your computer is properly hooked up
to a printer, of course (or that you have access to
someone else's printer).

INSTANT REVISIONS As you know, writing consists mostly of constant revising. On a typewriter, even a slick one, revising is an incredibly time-consuming procedure—it's tedious and imprecise, requiring lots of retyping to add or delete words and sentences and paragraphs. Adding or removing even just a couple of words can mean retyping entire pages. A PC converted to a word processor liberates you from retyping large sections of material every time you want to make a revision or correction; you make the changes smoothly on the electronic page that appears on your monitor. The electronic page automatically adjusts to accommodate deleted or inserted text. And once you've made your revisions, you can instruct the PC to print out the revised version.

Let's look at a simple example. Imagine that you have to write a one-page essay for a new job application. You're using a typewriter. Each time you write a new draft you have to retype the entire page. You've just finished what you thought was the final draft when you realize that you accidentally typed the same line twice in the middle of the page. Since you want the essay to look perfect, you have no choice but to retype the entire page . . . again. Ugh! What's worse, every time you retype, you risk introducing new errors.

Now imagine that you're writing this one-page essay with a word processor. You type (or "key in") the first draft onto the screen. To make changes you move words, sentences, paragraphs, whole blocks of text around anywhere in the electronic document, without retyping a single character and without resorting to scissors and glue. Likewise, you can insert new text at any location in your essay or delete text instantly. Word spacing and line spacing adjust automatically to accommodate any changes you make. In short, you can revise day and night without having to retype pages. Glory glory, hallelujah!

When you're done revising, you instruct your computer to print the copy on the printer, and there it is: perfection! Oh, but there's that line you somehow copied over twice in the middle of the letter. No sweat: Just zap the extra line on the screen. The remaining text in your essay adjusts automatically. Now you may instruct your PC to print another copy. This one really is perfect. It's a miracle: No retyping to accommodate revisions. This is a giant boon to efficiency.

APPLICATIONS
AND
ACTIVITIES:
GET WITH
THE
PROGRAM

23

INSTANT FORMATTING One of the most immediate benefits of word processing is the flexibility it allows you in *formatting*—arranging text on the page. You can set left and right margins, paragraph indents, line spacing, and other text characteristics in the wink of an eye. Ditto centering lines, paragraphs, or entire documents. And, of course, you may change your format in a jiffy. Naturally, you never have to retype to make format changes. If you don't like what you see, you can try something else. It only takes a few seconds.

ADDITIONAL BENEFITS There are more advantages to word processing. Most word processors offer special characters (foreign letters, mathematical and scientific symbols, bullets, underlines, super and subscripts, etc.) and a mix of typefaces, type sizes, and type styles. Creating footnotes, indexes, tables of contents is a cinch, as are running headers or footers with printed page numbers.

What's more, teamed up with an advanced, but not necessarily expensive printer, word processors print pages that look professionally typeset. (You can generate even more elaborate page designs by using a word processor in combination with a desktop publishing program; see page 51.)

CORRECTING ERRORS (INSTANTLY) Most word processors allow you to correct errors throughout a document instantly. If, for example, you're using a word processor and misspell someone's last name (it's Owen, not Owens) in a 20-page report where the name occurs 112 times, you can correct the spelling in *all* 112 occurrences throughout the 20 pages automatically without retyping. This takes mere seconds, and naturally, all the spaces adjust automatically to accommodate the correction. Consider what you'd have to do to correct 112 occurrences of a misspelled word in a 20-page document using a typewriter. *Have a nice life, friend.*

MASS MAILING Dear Friends . . . Dear Concerned Citizen . . . Dear Valued Client . . . If you ever send any kind of form letter—from end-of-the-year family newsletters to press releases to club, church, customer, constituent, or client correspondence—you can use your word processor to banish such turn-off salutations forever. Just be sure it contains a capability called *mail merge.* This feature allows you to automatically individualize the greeting ("Dear Tim and Kathy" instead of "Dear Friends") of a mass mailing. You can likewise customize other elements of the letter, from the lead paragraph to interior sentences to the sign-off and postscript. Not everyone needs mail merge, of course; but individuals and businesses that rely on mass mailings, if only once a year for holiday letters, are likely to find this feature worth the cost of the program many times over.

RESISTANCE AND REWARD People who write professionally for a living, especially creative writers like novelists and playwrights, are often reluctant and even fearful of changing the way they write. This is easy to understand. After all, creativity can be fleeting and fragile. The same instinct that leads some authors to do all their work at a favored desk with a familiar view at a particular time of day may lead them to insist on preserving their traditional method of writing.

Still, most people who write with any frequency, whether they correspond with friends and relatives, churn out annual reports and advertising copy, or sweat blood over novels and essays, embrace word processors once they've had a little experience with them.

If you spend more than a couple hours a week writing, you owe it to yourself to test-drive a word processor (see page 140 for tips on how to do this). This technology is not the future; it's very much the present. Once you've sat down at a word processor (more accurately: at a PC you've converted into a word processor with word processing application software), you're likely to come to the conclusion that retyping to make revisions is as archaic as rushing to the bank before three o'clock to stand in line for a teller every time you need cash.

Nonetheless, only wild-eyed Panglossians claim that word processors make people into good writers. They do not—no more so, in any case, than typewriters did when they replaced fountain pens. A word processor will certainly make you a more efficient writer. And it may help you become a better writer because it encourages you to rearrange words, move paragraphs around, see how certain words look and read together

—in short, to experiment. But in no way is it going to turn you into a witty Parker, a watchful Proust, or a wonderfully wretched Poe. You will still be you.

See also Desktop Publishing, page 51; Writing Aids, page 26; WYSIWYG, page 69.

**APPLICATIONS
AND
ACTIVITIES:
GET WITH
THE
PROGRAM**

25

WRITING AIDS

If you use a word processor, you should know about related applications. Sometimes these allied programs are
actually included with the word processor (check the list
of features on the word processor package). If not, they're
available separately. The most common of these is the
spelling checker, a program that automatically identifies
most misspelled words and typographical errors in documents created with a word processor.

The only way you can check and correct spelling and
typos in the absence of a spelling checker is to (1) read
the document word for word, (2) possess good enough
spelling sense to recognize suspect words when you see
them, and (3) look up every word you're unsure about in
the dictionary, or hire a copy editor. Spelling checkers are
not fail-safe, however. If you type *wand* instead of *want*,
most spelling checkers would not recognize the error because *wand* is a legitimate word, despite the fact that it's
not the intended word.

Other PC writing aids available include grammar
checkers, style guides, electronic dictionaries and thesauruses, and outliners, programs designed to help you structure your writing.

See also: Word Processors, page 21.

INSTRUCTIONAL PROGRAMS

APPLICATIONS
AND
ACTIVITIES:
GET WITH
THE
PROGRAM

27

Many applications are available for converting a personal computer into a tireless, challenging, and effective electronic study partner. It's no exaggeration to declare that the best instructional programs are even inspired, reflecting not only the subject expertise of their developers, but their love of learning and skill as teachers.

Of course, just as there are dreary, hidebound pedagogues in the world (and in everyone's personal experience), there are mediocre, dull instructional programs. This shouldn't surprise you; instructional software, after all, is only human.

The range of choice in subjects is impressive. Want to build your vocabulary, for example, or improve your spelling or sharpen your sense of place (geography)? The PC can help. Or how about dusting off your German, Spanish, Italian, Russian, Japanese, Latin, or French? Carpe diem, *mes amis*—seize the day, my friends. Or more to the point, seize the appropriate foreign language software.

If you're ready for more advanced instruction, check out advanced French, advanced German, advanced Spanish, etc. Bible studies software has been around since . . . the beginning, actually; it appeared almost simultaneously with the debut of personal computers. You can even skim the scriptures in Hebrew on a PC screen. Planning to take the SAT, GRE, or LSAT, or a host of other standard exams? The PC can be your study partner.

Instructional programs for young children are very common—and very popular—starting with preschoolers. These tend to be simple and friendly, often gamelike, emphasizing number, letter, color, and shape recognition and other skills appropriate to the age group.

Most educational programs for older children stay close to standard lessons: spelling, vocabulary, reading skills and comprehension, arithmetic, basic science, and so forth for grade-schoolers; algebra, geometry, calculus, biology, chemistry, and remedial studies for the higher grades. In addition, IBM and other companies have developed elaborate, much-praised PC-based curricula for teaching reading and writing to young children and for combating adult illiteracy. (IBM's phonetics-based approach is called "Writing to Read.")

See also: Training Software, page 59.

PROFESSIONAL AND SMALL BUSINESS/INTEGRATED APPLICATIONS

A confession: There really is no such thing as "professional and small business" software. Applications are almost always categorized by what they *do*, not by who they're *for*. Small business software is whatever small business uses: Word processors, for example, are almost always small business software; spreadsheets are often small business software; graphics applications may be small business software.

So what's the point? The point is that when you go into a software store you're likely to see a shelf marked . . . Small Business. And what you're likely to find on that shelf are *integrated packages.*

Integrated simply means that several mainstream applications have been rolled into one relatively inexpensive multipurpose product. Each application is called a *module.* Typically, the integrated "packages" include word processing, electronic spreadsheet, database management, and communications modules. Other facilities, including limited business graphics (chart- and graph-making), a spelling checker, dictionary and thesaurus, outliner, and desktop utilities, may also be included.

The integrated approach offers several advantages. First, by paying for one product with several applications instead of buying four or five separate applications, you save money. More important to many users, integration between applications enhances ease of use. The look and feel of the apps is similar from one application module to another; commands are consistent; and it's fairly easy to switch from one module to another or to transfer data—text, numbers, graphics—between modules.

Many small businesses favor integrated packages because, as they're relatively easy to use, employees need less training to get up and running with them. This quality is especially appealing in work environments new to personal computing. What the application modules in an integrated package gain in ease of use, however, they usually sacrifice in power—processing speed and capability —compared to stand-alone applications. Individuals and small businesses often don't require the bells and whistles of high-end stand-alone applications.

A number of other applications described separately in this section are of particular interest to small businesses and independent professionals. These include Money Managers, page 30, and Practice Management, page 46.

SELF-IMPROVEMENT/PERSONAL INTEREST

APPLICATIONS
AND
ACTIVITIES:
GET WITH
THE
PROGRAM

29

This catch-basin category is filled with inane, offbeat, practical, and inspired applications. Of course, what's inane to one person is inspired to another. So you be the judge. The products described here are but a sampling of the variety of choices available. Generally this category includes programs related to hobbies and special interests, personal fitness, questionable compulsions, and even ineradicable self-delusions.

Personally, I don't think there's anything inane about genealogical programs designed to help you trace your family tree. Just don't expect them to do your research for you. They're mostly fill-in-the-blank templates, electronic versions of old-fashioned "find your ancestor" kits.

Sports handicapping software and casino training programs (especially blackjack) may inspire nothing but yawns among nongamblers, but others will jump at the chance to cover their bets. Fine, but Lotto enhancement software? (A fool and his money . . .) Or, if you're one of those poor, bedeviled creatures incapable of decompressing in one of the million or so methods already available to our species, usually at no cost, you may be a candidate for relaxation software. If, however, your problem is a lack of stimulation, you might want to consider adults-only software (one of these products is called Se*XX*y). If you're in the mood to "take control of your life," how about a nutrition program that analyzes your diet and makes personalized recommendations based on your age, weight, and fitness profile?

MONEY MANAGERS

Whether you're a free-spirited wage earner unburdened by debt or dependents, who owns no property and claims no deductions, or you are the senior bean counter at Lucre-Lust, Inc., there's probably an off-the-shelf money manager software package for you. At least there's a money manager that claims to be just for you. Personal computers have thoroughly infiltrated the bill-paying, buck-tracking, bean-counting, bottom-line-divining racket, personal and otherwise.

This is mostly for the good, but in some cases PC-based money management applications amount to over-kill. Yes, you certainly can buy a program that will track your cash flow, assign expenses to categories you define, and print checks, but does this make sense if you file a short income tax form once a year and write no more than half-a-dozen personal checks each month? In a word: no.

Personal and small business money management programs are usually inexpensive (under $100), packed with clever and useful capabilities, and are relatively easy to use. They typically provide some tax planning and preparation features. One popular program, Quicken, for example, tracks bank accounts (checking, savings, money market, etc.), credit cards, cash, assets (certificates of deposit, mutual funds, investments, capital equipment, etc.), and liabilities (loans and mortgages).

Quicken generates too many kinds of reports to list here, but a sampling includes cash flow, monthly budget, itemized categories, account balances, and customized reports. A "bill-minder" function actually reminds you when bills are due. You can generate profit-and-loss statements, accounts payable by vendor, accounts receivable by customer, payroll, and balance sheet summaries. Pretty nifty, but not necessarily the best personal and small business financial program for everyone's purposes. Ask around. Do a little homework. Then decide what's best for you.

PERSONAL INFORMATION MANAGERS (PIMs)

APPLICATIONS
AND
ACTIVITIES:
GET WITH
THE
PROGRAM

31

The average desk is cluttered with stuff: a datebook, an address file, a clock, memo paper, various reminders ("Make Haircut Appointment!" or "Dad's Birthday Next Week!" or "Cancel Tuesday Staff Meeting"), possibly one of those "Word-a-Day" or "Inspiration-a-Day" calendars, a calculator, and any number of other workaday accoutrements.

These and other handy desk mates are available on disk in *pop-up* facilities known as *personal information managers* or *PIMs*. Pop-up simply means that you can make any one of these accessories appear on the monitor in its own miniscreen, or *window*, right in the middle of whatever application you're using. The idea is to make the on-screen desktop version of these tools every bit as handy as the graspable ones you're used to.

Different PIMs offer different collections of accessories, so be sure to look them over carefully. If, for example, you spend a lot of time on the phone, you'll want an autodialer, phone log, and appointment scheduler. At least one PIM even calculates fees based on your hourly rate and the time you spend on the phone with clients.

ENTERTAINMENT

As far as many PC users are concerned, the theme song for their machines isn't "Got Work to Do" so much as "Let Me Entertain You." To which one can only add, "Let Me Count the Ways."

Actually, there are too many ways to count. But most of the hundreds of adult, adolescent, and children's games and other amusements available for personal computers do fall into five categories: *arcade-style* games, *fantasy role-playing* games, *adaptations* of board games and TV game shows, *simulations*, and *action/adventure games*.

Not every PC game fits neatly into one category or another. Some are exactly what they seem to be; others are all over the map. So if you've got your pounding little heart set on a blood-boiling action/adventure game, for example, be sure to read the label carefully before opening the package. Better yet, try before you buy (see page 140).

All PC-based games are not created equal. In some cases the concept is flawed. Some suffer from poor design, shoddy graphics, or other forms of terminal neglect, including awkward commands and slow responses. More than a few computer games, echoing trends in television and other realms of unreal life, are unapologetically disgusting. A growing number of fleshy or particularly violent PC games are not appropriate for children (if anyone). There's no formal rating system, although some publishers of "adults only" entertainment software voluntarily label their products accordingly.

Many computer games, though, are clever, engaging (at least for a while), and in their own way, pretty. The more technically sophisticated ones are dazzlingly spectacular, especially if you have a PC with a high-resolution and color monitor and decent sound reproduction technology.

Typically, PC games allow solo play (against the computer) as well as either simultaneous or sequential competition between two or more human players. Fantasy role-playing games, which are really long, solitary interactive novels, are frequently an exception.

Most games allow you to adjust the level of difficulty. Some allow you to halt a game in progress, turn off the machine, and resume later where you left off. Automatic scoring is virtually standard, and many games automatically maintain and display various kinds of game-to-game tallies like "Ten Best Scores/Players."

ARCADE-STYLE GAMES Arcade-style games are electronic knockoffs of traditional pinball games and other arcade favorites. They emphasize quick response, eye-hand coordination, and other motor skills. The best ones are simple but ingenious, appealing to the mind as well as the brain stem. Not surprisingly, many arcade-style computer games attract mainly kids and young adults, no doubt because youthful synapses still work well. Arcade-style games work best if you've got a mouse or a control device called a joystick (see page 89). Warning: This category can be horribly—or wonderfully, depending on your outlook—mesmerizing, regardless of your age. Approach with caution.

FANTASY ROLE-PLAYING GAMES These games are pure invention, usually populated with fire-breathing dragons, enchanted sorceresses, mutating gnomes, and the like. You, the player, are given a near-impossible mission, or quest. Before setting out through a long series of episodes, you select companions, weapons, personal strengths and weaknesses, and magical powers. The monitor displays text explaining your situation and what's expected of you in each episode. You're constantly called upon to make life-and-death decisions, solve riddles, interpret strange or ominous omens, translate bizarre messages, and duel unspeakably horrible creatures. If you fail to do the right thing, you're made to suffer by losing personal powers, a limb or two, or even your on-screen life.

The best fantasy role-playing games are imaginative and dynamic; they display maps and other aids, depict scenes from different perspectives, incorporate animation, and imbue characters with the ability to adjust to experience. Most fantasy role-playing games take forever to play. This is no impediment to those who still enjoy the sweet delusion that life itself goes on forever—mainly the under-twenty crowd.

ADAPTATIONS Game adaptations don't need a lot of explaining. These days you can buy PC versions of chess, bridge, poker, trivia, Jeopardy!, Wheel of Fortune, Scrabble, cribbage, Risk, pinochle, and a whole lot of other familiar and not-so-familiar parlor game choices.

Many adaptations are just plain terrific, offering the means via PC to play favorite TV or parlor games even when no one human is around to play with you.

APPLICATIONS
AND
ACTIVITIES:
GET WITH
THE
PROGRAM

33

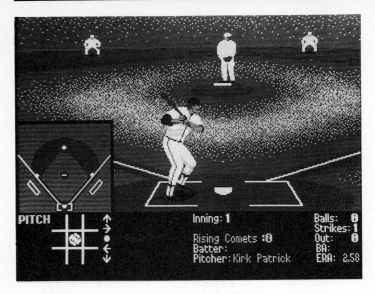

PITCH

Inning: **1**

Rising Comets :**0**
Batter:
Pitcher: Kirk Patrick

Balls: **0**
Strikes: **1**
Out: **0**
BA:
ERA: 2.58

Hardball II™ **is a good example of a simulation game.** (Photo courtesy of Accolade.)

Alas, some adaptations fall short because in adapting them to the PC, their developers made too many technical compromises that result in awkward commands, excruciatingly slow play, inferior graphics, or poor handling of multiple players. So, as with all applications software, don't make any assumptions; when in doubt, check it out.

SIMULATIONS Simulations offer players the chance to be a vicarious race car driver, fighter pilot, submarine commander, air traffic controller, professional baseball manager or player, football quarterback, or any of dozens of other glory-seeking overachievers. They put you right in the driver's seat, on the pitcher's mound, or wherever. If you're a fighter pilot, for example, the screen simulates the view from the cockpit, including a working control panel. You manipulate your jet and its weapons by entering commands. Out the simulated cockpit window, the enemy sweeps down for the attack, growing larger as it approaches your plane. Your job is that of any well-trained fighter pilot in this situation: Think fast or die. Fortunately, if you do die, you can immediately *un*die and start all over again.

Early simulations suffered from jerky animation, grainy graphics, and unbelievable perspectives. With improvements in computer programming techniques and hardware, simulations have gotten better and better. Today, many games in this category appeal to adults as much as to teenagers. These include team sport adaptations, the best of which have been lovingly conceived and developed by skilled game designers and programmers who are also passionate fans of the sport. They're designed to allow you to do all kinds of magical things like mix and match famous players and replay notable real-life games.

ACTION/ADVENTURE GAMES Action/adventure games may emphasize role-playing, arcade effects, simulation, all of the above, or none of the above. In other words, this is a scattershot, little-bit-of-this, little-bit-of-that category.

Many action/adventure games are adaptations of popular novels *(The Hunt for Red October)* and movies *(Nightmare on Elm Street)*, often of the white-knuckle, blood-and-guts, shoot-'em-up (or beam-'em-up) variety. They may also be based on historical events (World War II is a big favorite), inexhaustibly popular themes (international espionage), and even scientific discoveries (the search for the *Titanic*).

Action/adventure games typically incorporate aspects of fantasy role-playing games. Some, though, have more in common with arcade-style games and simple, if automated, board games.

APPLICATIONS
AND
ACTIVITIES:
GET WITH
THE
PROGRAM

35

DATABASE MANAGEMENT SYSTEMS

Database Management Systems are also called *DBMS software* or simply, *databases*, as in "What kind of database do you use?" In ordinary terms a database is nothing more than an organized collection of information. An address book, for example, is a database. So are a recipe file, a zip code directory, and even a dictionary. When you hand your credit card to a store clerk and he uses it to check your available credit over the phone lines, he's consulting a database. In one form or another, these storehouses of information are everywhere.

PC databases are electronic versions of information receptacles like file cabinets, hanging folders, and manila files—except that file cabinets are passive, and PC databases are dynamic as lightning. They make adding, deleting, and altering information a snap because you do such work on the computer screen. But there's more to PC databases than efficient data entry and revision.

LIMITS OF TRADITIONAL FILING SYSTEMS To understand the advantages of an electronic database, imagine a paper, or mechanical, database, consisting of high school filing cabinets filled with records for 2000 students. When you want information from these files, you have to remove it according to the strict scheme in which the files were originally organized, most likely in alphabetical order by last name.

This is no problem if all you want to do is locate the Cleaver file or the Morimoto file or the Rodriguez file. But suppose the state health agency wants a list of students who were absent due to flu last year. Or the education department wants to know how many twin girls from families with incomes over $30,000 dropped out of school.

You see the problem. Extracting such information from an entire card file or filing cabinet requires a sophisticated system of parallel files and cross-referencing—and lots and lots of time.

Electronic databases eliminate the need for parallel files, cross-referencing, and lots and lots of time. They offer unparalleled flexibility in managing information. With a database, for example, you can call up (display on the monitor) complete individual files, or *records*, as they're called (Cleaver or Morimoto or Rodriguez). Or you can instruct the program to spew out a list of names based on a particular criterion, or *field*, in data-

APPLICATIONS
AND
ACTIVITIES:
GET WITH
THE
PROGRAM

37

base lingo (names of all students absent due to flu last year). With high-end *relational databases* you can conduct searches through the database records based on a combination of criteria. You can, for example, instruct the program to give you a list of female twins (this is one field) from families with incomes over $30,000 (field 2) who dropped out of school (field 3). Imagine what you would have to do to locate such a list from a conventional paper-bound filing system. Of course, you can, at any point, print information extracted from electronic databases.

That's one example. There are thousands upon thousands of other uses for these PC marvels, ranging from personal to small business to institutional to corporate. But before you invest in a sophisticated electronic database management program, be sure you really need one. A proper address book or Rolodex is as sophisticated a database as most people need. If you think you can use a database, be sure to educate yourself about the differences between individual products before you buy, as they vary greatly in price, complexity, and ease of use.

A closing note: PC databases do not eliminate the need for filing cabinets, because not everything can or should be stored electronically. Magazine and newspaper clippings, brochures, signature-bearing documents, and legal papers, for example, often need to be preserved in their original form.

See also: Professional and Small Business/Integrated Applications, page 28; Application Enhancers, page 63.

ELECTRONIC SPREADSHEETS

If you've ever seen a mileage table or a teacher's grade-book or one of those campground guides that uses big dots to tell you which camps have running water, trailer hookups, life-guards at the beach, and built-in barbecue grills, you've seen a spreadsheet. In the raw, spreadsheets are simple grids on paper, composed of little boxes, or *cells*, each containing a bit of information.

People have been using paper spreadsheets for hundreds of years to organize, store, and present information—in particular, financial information—and for making calculations.

SIMPLE SPREADSHEETS For organizing and presenting information (as in the campground guide), electronic spreadsheets offer the same time-saving convenience of word processors. You can make revisions—add, delete, and rearrange information—on the screen. You can even insert or remove columns and rows; the grid adjusts automatically to all revisions. When you're satisfied with what you've wrought, you can print the spreadsheet.

MULTIPLE CALCULATIONS The real wonder of spreadsheets, though, is how they handle numerical information. To understand why, let's step back to a paper ledger. Suppose that you own a six-unit apartment building. To keep track of the income and expenses, you pencil rent and deposit, upkeep, and repair information into a paper ledger. You add across the columns to figure your total collections and outlays for each month. At the end of the year, you add the totals. Simple enough, even by hand on preprinted paper grids.

But let's say you own 100 buildings. Or that you have 200 employees and need to calculate payroll taxes, social security taxes, and annual raises, and so forth. To manage this kind of complex data on paper is an incredibly time-consuming and error-prone experience, not to mention sight-robbing and spirit-sapping.

Until recently, however, manual recording was the only way to do it. Poor wretches spent their working lives sharpening pencil stubs, doing individual calculations on scrap paper or in their heads, and entering each one in the endless cells of a paper spreadsheet. If they failed to catch mistakes soon enough, they risked contaminating the whole spreadsheet with errors. The horror! The horror!

Mechanical adding machines and later, electronic calculators, helped automate the process and reduce errors, but the unfortunate drudges who used them were still limited to doing calculations one-by-one.

PC-based electronic spreadsheets, however, allow you to calculate across an entire grid automatically. Better yet, they allow you to alter your data and recalculate in short order—again and again if you want—all on the screen. When you're satisfied with the result, you can print the spreadsheet.

"WHAT IF?" CALCULATIONS This electronic versatility comes in especially handy when you want to make What if calculations. What if calculations are common to many professions. Business partners, for example, planning to borrow money to launch a new whirligig assembly plant, might ask themselves questions like, "What if we pay 25 cents instead of 27 cents per gizmo and 81 cents rather than 84 cents per widget?" And "What if we hold your labor costs to 44 percent of sales and our advertising costs to 19 percent of sales, instead of 50 percent and 23 percent respectively?" And so on . . .

This is a bare-bones example, but it's enough to give you an idea of how complex and overwhelming What if calculations can become. Real entrepreneurs planning to open a real whirligig assembly plant would play variations of What if until long after the cows come home. The idea is to refine the business concept on paper (or on the screen) before trying to make it work in the real world.

Entrepreneurs are not the only people who create What if scenarios. Scientists and engineers; accountants; marketing and salespeople; medical researchers; stock and bond traders; personnel managers; rate setters for airlines, insurance, taxes, interest, and just about everything on the planet that's the least bit subject to rate setting; meteorologists; statisticians; census takers; pollsters and demographers; and a surprisingly big chunk of the rest of humanity also play What if.

You don't have to be a calculating fool to appreciate spreadsheets, though. Anyone whose work requires making and filling grids (tables), even if you fill them with descriptive text rather than numbers, will appreciate what an electronic spreadsheet can do.

See also: Application Enhancers, page 63.

COMMUNICATIONS/ELECTRONIC MAIL/FAX

No PC is an island. No PC stands alone. At least, no PC is forced to stand alone if you have three things: communications software, a hardware device called a *modem* (rhymes with totem), and a phone line.

By commandeering phone lines to forge a communications link, you can use your PC to send and receive text—anything from sweet nothings to 200-page (or longer) documents—to and from another PC across the room or around the world. Properly equipped, you may also send and receive other forms of data besides text, including electronic spreadsheets. In some cases, you can even receive applications.

ELECTRONIC MAIL PC communications is a vast subject and it can be quite complicated. Fortunately, the most useful form of PC communications, *electronic mail*, or *E-Mail*, is readily available, offers lots of options, and is usually quite easy to use. The only hitch: You have to subscribe to an E-Mail service. Like phone companies, E-Mail companies charge various fees based on which particular features of the service you use, based on hookup time, or both.

E-Mail allows you to sit at your PC, write a message or memo or novel with a word processor, and transmit them in a twinkling—well, the novel would need longer than a twinkling—over phone lines. If your intended recipient is a fellow subscriber to the same E-Mail service, your missive will be deposited in his *electronic mailbox* as soon as the transmission is completed. At any time of day or night, the recipient can use his PC to check his mailbox for messages. (Most E-Mail users check their mailboxes at least once a day.) When he finds your message, your recipient can read it on his monitor, save it on floppy or hard disk, print it, or do all three. He may also send an instant reply to *your* electronic mailbox. Some services even allow E-Mail correspondents to forward messages electronically to other recipients.

What if your intended recipient doesn't have a PC or isn't a subscriber to the same E-Mail service? You can send your message to a fax machine or a telex via E-Mail. If your recipient doesn't have a fax or telex, you can instruct E-Mail to convert your electronic message to a paper message at a site near the recipient and deliver it through the U.S. Post Office.

If you want, you can send the same message to ten recipients (or any number), specifying how you want the message delivered (electronic, fax, telex, paper) for each destination. No bothering with paper and envelopes and stamps. No telephone tag. E-Mail is a great boon to efficiency, especially for business.

ON-LINE SERVICES E-Mail companies not only serve as a conduit for sending and receiving text and other kinds of data, they also offer, for a fee, access to *on-line services*: weather information, stock quotes from Wall Street, airline schedules, current news off the wire, and even text transmitted electronically from back issues of prominent newspapers and magazines (see "Information Searches," page 44). Subscribers also use on-line services to post messages or to read electronic bulletin boards (see below); to seek technical assistance; to exchange want ads, including personals; and to hold conferences with other far-flung subscribers. On-line services are also available independently of E-Mail companies. Some computer magazines, for example, offer articles, utilities (little PC enhancement programs), technical advice, access to editors and other offerings via PC and phone line.

Many individuals, associations, and institutions sponsor *electronic bulletin boards*. These are similar to E-Mail services except that instead of providing private electronic mailboxes, they provide the PC equivalent of a public notice board. You gain access to the board over phone lines and scan notices, announcements, and messages on your monitor. You can, of course, post notices, announcements, etc., as well as remove them (actually, you don't remove them; you use your PC to make instant electronic copies). Electronic bulletin boards are often created to serve groups with shared interests—bird-watchers, for example, or veterans or physicists.

PC-TO-PC: DIRECT LINKS There's no law of science that says you must use a middleman—an E-Mail service—to link up with other personal computers. People commonly use communications software to forge independent links over phone lines for exchanging text and other kinds of data. You may also employ independent links to operate your PC or remove data from it from afar; naturally you need a PC at your end to practice this rarefied form of PC communications called *re-*

mote access. Finally, you can use direct links to "Let your fingers do the talking." As you type on your keyboard, your words appear simultaneously on your monitor and on the monitor at the other end of the phone line; likewise, your conversation partner's words appear simultaneously on his or her monitor and yours. By taking turns, you can have a conversation without opening your mouth.

NETWORKS All of the PC communication linkups described so far depend on telephone lines, which offer an unparalleled advantage: worldwide access. With communications software, a modem, and a phone line, you can use your PC to send a message to Memphis, a telex to Tanzania, a fax to Frankfurt, and vice versa. This is fine and good. But using commercial E-Mail services and telephone lines to communicate with PCs on the same floor or in the same building is a little ridiculous—and unnecessary. It's unnecessary, that is, if the PCs are cabled together in a closed circuit network, better known as a *local area network (LAN,* rhymes with pan).

Local area networks provide internal E-Mail to groups sharing a work space—an office building, for example, or the floor of an office building, or the corner of a floor of an office building, or even a home office. Many companies use LAN-based internal E-Mail to pass work from one department to another, as well as for sending messages to one another. Users on the network may still communicate with the outside world via commercial E-Mail services.

LANs also give PC users equal access to printers and other hardware, as well as to shared databases, and even to applications, many of which are designed especially for groups working together rather than for individual users. Sharing hardware and other resources over the network can increase efficiency and save money. A small business with fifteen employees, for example, each with a personal computer, could link all the employees to a single high-end (and expensive) laser printer rather than investing in an individual printer for each employee. The employees can use the network to send data to the printer from their desktop PCs. They don't, in other words, have to get up, walk to the printer, and stand around waiting. They may continue working at their desks until the printing is completed.

Local area networks are changing the face of business. But they are complex facilities, often requiring technical expertise to install. Large LANs frequently require an expert manager to oversee the network and help users with questions and problems.

See also: Information Searches, page 44; Modems, page 100.

APPLICATIONS
AND
ACTIVITIES:
GET WITH
THE
PROGRAM

43

INFORMATION SEARCHES

The PC has become a significant research tool for journalists and writers, attorneys, doctors, scientists, students, businesspeople, and just about anyone whose work requires sifting through volumes of printed material—books, newspapers, company records, inventory information, and so forth. There are two ways to turn personal computers into information search tools: through on-line services and by using a CD-ROM reader. CD-ROM stands for compact disk read-only memory, what most of us call simply CDs.

ON-LINE RESEARCH With communications software and a modem, you can examine everything from current and back issues of newspapers, magazines, and journals, to vast legal libraries, encyclopedias, and statistics on just about anything, right on your monitor. The convenience of sitting in front of your PC monitor and electronically searching at remarkable speed through ten years of the *New York Times* or other sources doesn't come cheap, however. It's not surprising, then, that most people who do research on-line do so when the company or client is footing the bill.

CD-ROM (MASS STORAGE) Huge quantities of information— from *The Complete Works of William Shakespeare* and the Bible to corporate data and years' worth of magazine issues—can be stored on compact disks. You know . . . CDs, like the shiny plastic ones used to hold recordings of Mahler and Madonna.

And just as a CD player can "read" CD recordings of Madonna, PCs working in tandem with a *CD-ROM reader* can read the bard, the Bible, and other material stored on *ROM disks,* as they're often called.

"So what?" you say. You can read the Bible just as easily in old-fashioned book form? This is true, but what if you want to track down the source of an ob- scure quote you dimly recall from Sunday school days? Yes, you could spend hours or weeks searching for it in the Good Book—or you could type the quote, or a fragment of it, into your PC and let your CD-ROM reader track it down in seconds.

There are even greater possibilities, for the tech- nology already exists to combine text and other forms of data with sights (video) and sounds (audio) on CD- ROM. Commercial products that exploit this technol- ogy are already available, though they are expensive. Before long, however, you'll be able to buy an encyclo- pedia on disk, call up "Mahler," and read the entry, listen to selections from Mahler symphonies, and watch turn-of-the-century film clips of the composer strolling in Bohemia, all on your personal computer— and for a reasonable price.

See also CD-ROM Readers, page 102; Communica- tions, page 40.

PRACTICE MANAGEMENT

Question: What do doctors and dentists in private practice, gardeners, masseurs and masseuses, counselors, property managers, car repair shop owners, accountants, therapists, lawyers, contractors, nurse practitioners, astrologers, supervisors of ministorage facilities, church secretaries, managers of preschools, architects, and physical therapists have in common?

Answer: They can all benefit from applications designed expressly to help run people-oriented and service-oriented businesses. These practice management programs are designed to automate many, if not all, of the tasks related to running independent businesses, including personnel records, expenses, time billing, and cash flow.

Some practice management applications are targeted at particular trades and professions. There are, for example, PC programs designed to manage the patient accounts of medical and dental practices—billing, appointment reminders, etc. There are also construction cost-control programs and commercial, residential, condo, and even ministorage facility property management programs. There's a home owner association management program and tenant tracking programs and programs designed for overseeing church income and expenses. And lots more.

One of the greatest needs of independent consultants and free-lancers is an efficient, methodical approach to itemizing, calculating, and invoicing billable time and expenses. A number of programs specializing in this task are available. So if you're in the business of equating seconds and minutes with nickels and dimes, it might be worth your time to check out the possibilities.

GRAPHICS

APPLICATIONS
AND
ACTIVITIES:
GET WITH
THE
PROGRAM

47

Rugged old verities are falling left and right, but at least one seems to grow only stronger: A picture is worth a thousand words. This indestructible truth has inspired many hardware and software wizards to devote whole careers to the picture-making side of personal computers. The result: PCs are not only text-processing and number-crunching machines; they're also impressively versatile picture-making machines.

PC graphics applications are used for everything from idle (but fun) doodling to illustrating personal correspondence and newsletters to creating fully realized works of art. They're also used widely in business to illustrate memos, reports, and presentations.

"Picture" can mean just about anything in PC Land, from skimpy, crude black-on-white bar charts to luscious thousand-color compositions. But don't jump to the conclusion that all you have to do is buy a PC, key in a few commands (or draw a few lines using a mouse), and sit back waiting for the chief of acquisitions from the Louvre to call.

In the first place, many graphics applications require special hardware. More important, using them to good effect requires know-how—and not just usual kid-genius wires-and-pliers hacker variety of PC know-how. Besides, just as word processors can't make nonwriters or bad writers into good writers, PC graphics programs cannot make nonartists into artists.

On the other hand, the whole point of hundreds of graphics programs is to give nonartists the ability to create high-quality, professional-looking images, if not art, exactly. For this reason, graphics is not only an interesting applications category to most users, it's an important, even vital one. PC graphics programs offer tools offered nowhere else. As for artists, graphics programs open up new worlds of creative opportunities for those graced with artistic ability.

PC-created images may either stand alone or be combined with text and other images. They can usually be printed with standard black-and-white or color PC printers, though print quality varies greatly depending on the complexity of the image and the sophistication of the printer. When the printing job is complex or only the highest print standards will do, graphical work created with PCs may be sent on a floppy disk to professional printers (including some local copy shops) to be produced.

Printing isn't the only way to exhibit PC-created graphics. Images may also be displayed on monitors and converted to transparencies (for overhead projectors), 35 mm slides, photographic prints, and even videotape.

CHARTS AND GRAPHS One of the most common categories of PC graphics applications is *chart- and graph-making* programs. These provide a relatively quick, cheap, and easy way to transform unwieldy information or inert, sleep-inducing numbers (sales this quarter up 17 percent from last quarter in comparison to a decline of 6 percent during the same period last year) into sprightly, captivating pictures.

Most chart- and graph-making programs do the drawing for you, creating images from numerical data you give them. Ideal for business, they're also useful for schools, hospitals, associations of all kinds, nonprofits—anyone with a story to tell in numbers.

Programs are also available for creating nonnumerical organizational charts, decision trees, and any number of related graphical presentations.

MAP PROGRAMS Off-the-shelf map programs provide predrawn maps you can customize to suit your needs. You could, for example, "call up" a map of North America. Then you could use the program to mark off your company's sales territories. Within each territory you could designate the location of sales outlets or branch offices and further annotate the map with text, numerical data, or other graphical images.

Map programs may be used by anyone, but they've found their greatest following, not surprisingly, from business users. Different programs contain different maps, map scales (some provide a choice of scales), and capabilities.

FREEHAND DRAW AND PAINT PROGRAMS Without doubt, the most all-round fun graphics applications are the *freehand draw or paint programs*. These provide a number of sophisticated tools that allow you to sketch; create patterns; and duplicate, reposition, or reverse images on screen. They're amazingly agile, and to many users, endlessly seductive, if only for doodling. Most of them include a capacity for mixing in text in different typefaces, type styles, and sizes. Of course, you can store

APPLICATIONS
AND
ACTIVITIES:
GET WITH
THE
PROGRAM

49

your creations on disk or print them or, in many cases, incorporate them in other text or graphics files, including presentation graphics compositions.

Professional artists and designers use more advanced paint programs to convert their PCs to electronic canvases. Depending on native talent and technical knowledge, artists can create electronic paintings that are fully realized works of art—surprisingly textural and emotionally moving, as successful paintings always are.

Electronic painters are not necessarily interested in creating emotionally moving pictures, though. Many use professional paint programs and related software to create commercial art, from advertisements and brochures to posters and album covers.

PRESENTATION GRAPHICS   Many people are interested in only one kind of graphics application, programs geared to creating projected images (via monitor, slide projector, or overhead projector). These are used to illustrate lectures, business meetings, product introductions, and other formal presentations.

The most sophisticated of these presentation graphics programs help assure design consistency from one image to the next. Many include facilities for creating related printed material to hand out during presentations.

ELECTRONIC CLIP ART   The story you want to tell with pictures may have more to do with images of real things —trees, houses, people—than with prosaic charts and graphs. Such images are readily available to PC users through *electronic clip art*, predrawn, ready-to-print pictures of every imaginable kind.

There's nothing new about the concept of clip art; it's been around on paper since da Vinci was an apprentice. What's new is that it now comes on disk, so you can use a personal computer to copy an image—a tree, for example—combine it with text or other graphic elements if you want, and print it.

Clip art is usually sold in either all-purpose (a little bit of everything) or thematic collections, or *libraries*, as they're called. Thematic clip art libraries run the gamut from common everyday images (household items: refrigerator, desk lamp, welcome mat, etc.) to the specialized (military hardware: tanks, howitzers, battleships, etc.).

Clip art libraries are not true applications—they're data. Applications contain processing instructions, the ability to create or change data. Clip art libraries are merely inert collections of images stored on disk. That's okay, though, because you can use other graphics or desktop publishing (see page 51) programs to manipulate the images.

STOLEN IMAGES   There are three ways to get graphics into the personal computer: Create them from scratch (paint and draw programs), use ready-made images on disk (electronic clip art, map programs, etc.), and steal them from a tangible source: a snapshot, a newspaper illustration, an original pen-and-ink drawing, and so forth.

Well, maybe "steal" is too strong a word. The more conventional and appropriate (because the process is not inherently illegal) verb is *import*. Whatever you call the process, the fact remains that hardware peripherals called *scanners* and related software are widely available for transferring both images *and* text to the computer.

Once you've transferred images to the PC, you can see them on the monitor, store them on a floppy or hard disk, print them, project them, alter them, or all of the above. Most PC users, though, import text and graphics in order to incorporate them into printed materials (newsletters, magazines, press releases, announcements, brochures, etc.) and projected presentations (slide shows, etc.).

If you have appropriate graphics software, you can even edit imported images. You could, for example, add or change colors; you can also move elements of the image around (if it's a face, you might be fanciful —or spiteful—and turn the nose upside down or erase the ears, or you could be kind and remove the crow's feet from around the eyes).

Scanners are hardware devices, not applications. The process of scanning—importing—images, however, greatly extends the graphic possibilities of the PC. It's a way of bringing all the world's pictures into the machine, where you, the user, can use them as you will.

See also: Computer-aided Design, page 61; Desktop Publishing, page 51; Scanners, page 90.

DESKTOP PUBLISHING

APPLICATIONS
AND
ACTIVITIES:
GET WITH
THE
PROGRAM

51

Desktop publishing (DTP) is the synthesis of two applications—word processing and graphics. As such, it's used to design *and* produce anything that can be printed: newspapers, magazines, advertisements, posters, catalogs, menus, annual reports, soup can labels, greeting cards, and so forth. DTP allows you to take raw text and dress it up in a thousand different ways, changing typefaces, design elements, and layouts at will, among other things.

In some circles, desktop publishing is considered an application for graphic artists, production editors, and other design and publishing professionals *only,* end of discussion. While it's true that DTP has altered the work of professional designers and production editors who create design-intensive, or heavily formatted publications, desktop publishing applications also come in forms suitable for everyday users.

DESKTOP PUBLISHING FOR EVERYONE Some of the most delightful and generally useful DTP applications are also the most inexpensive, all-around accessible, and even fun. Many clubs, schools, civic organizations, church congregations, institutions, businesses, arts groups, and other associations, for example, publish their own newsletters. Typically these require ridiculous amounts of time to produce, and the results are frequently amateurish. A newsletter-oriented DTP program won't make it any easier to extract copy from contributors, but it does streamline production and can add polish to homegrown pages. Plus, you don't need to be an artist to dress up the newsletter since you can copy images from any of dozens of electronic clip art libraries available.

Inexpensive DTP programs are also available for designing personalized greeting cards for any occasion, banners, announcements, events programs, schedules, fact sheets, and other everyday publications. Some of the programs available for creating customized stationery and other paper products are especially appealing to children.

PROFESSIONAL DESKTOP PUBLISHING When most of us look at a printed page, even a simple one that appears to contain nothing but text, we don't see all the work that went into its design. Someone somewhere thought long and hard about that page. How wide should the columns of text be? What typeface should be used for the title? How about the subtitle and other special text? What about type sizes and spaces between lines? Should the right margin be ragged or straight? How much white space should there be? What about rules (black lines) between columns or for boxing in all the type?

That just about . . . scratches the surface. No kidding; a very ordinary, straightforward page can involve dozens of decisions by a professional graphic designer. Adding photographs, other images, or color to the page only increases the design decisions involved—and the complexity of the job.

Traditionally, graphic designers work with pencil and paper, rulers, X-Acto knives, and strips of print-ready type called repro to compose layouts on stiff pieces of cardboard. The galleys must be ordered from typographers, who use expensive, very specialized and precise typesetting equipment to produce them. In the process of taking a design from concept to final layout, designers may have to order type from typographers several times, usually waiting at least overnight for each order to be filled. And, of course, there's a charge for each order.

A personal computer, desktop publishing application software, and a high-end laser printer can greatly reduce, and in some cases even eliminate, a graphic designer's dependence on typesetters. Designers can use these tools to do many of the things they formerly depended on typographers to do for them: select different typefaces, size the type, change the word and line spacing, and so forth. Instead of composing layouts by pasting down galleys, designers can create the layouts electronically on the monitor.

Designers can also use a hardware device called a scanner to "import" photographs and illustrations to their electronic layouts. Increasingly, they can even use PCs to mix colors. Once they've composed a page with the PC they can print it on a high-resolution laser printer or send the page on disk to a printer.

By becoming less dependent on typesetters and other suppliers, graphic artists gain flexibility and control. Many designers emphasize these values over any savings in time and money when discussing the advantages of desktop publishing. In any case, desktop publishing is transforming the graphic design and publishing industry—from the local neighborhood shopping guide to slick national magazines.

ACCOUNTING

APPLICATIONS
AND
ACTIVITIES:
GET WITH
THE
PROGRAM

53

Accounting programs are not for the innumerate (innumeracy is to numbers what illiteracy is to letters). So if you're numbers-shy, don't imagine for a nanosecond that these programs have the power to change dull or threatening figures into raindrops on roses or whiskers on kittens. Ain't no such magic.

And for the most part, off-the-shelf PC-based accounting programs are not for individuals; they're for small- and midsized businesses that have moved beyond single-entry bookkeeping. Yes, there are money management as well as tax planning and preparation programs for ordinary folk, and these can be helpful, but such low-end capabilities—those oriented to individuals and smaller small businesses—tend to congregate more in the money management category described on page 30. Besides, *money management and tax planning and preparation* are not the same as *accounting*.

Accounting is heavy-duty stuff, a specialty. PC accounting applications are for specialists, for the people who know the difference between GAAP and GLAPPAR, and whose working vocabulary includes such fetching phrases as "force zero proof option" and "sunk costs." This does not necessarily mean you have to be a professional accountant to use a PC-based accounting program, but you've got to be familiar with the vocabulary and the procedures, no question about it. GAAP, incidentally, is shorthand for Generally Accepted Accounting Principles. GLAPPAR is explained below.

Dozens of accounting programs, of wildly uneven quality, clutter the market. The best inspire hosannas and get used, used, used; the worst take up shelf space in cramped offices or get donated to fledgling high school computer departments where they . . . take up shelf space.

Rare is the accounting program that does not offer general ledger, accounts payable, and accounts receivable (GLAPPAR). These may all come in one software package (though on several disks) or they may be sold as separate *modules*, so that you're not forced to pay for capabilities you don't need. Other common accounting functions available for PCs include inventory, purchase ordering, payroll, billing, and forecasting.

PC-based accounting systems, if wisely selected, offer abundant advantages, from better tracking of company cash flow to standardization of payables and receivables. They can alert you sooner than otherwise to the need to borrow money or of opportunities to invest excess funds. Spinoffs from better cash management and more consistent and comprehensive financial reporting may include better access to credit, lower tax liabilities, and more meaningful sales and break-even analyses. This is the short list. These programs also offer greater in-house control, easier access to data, and improved data security than time-sharing plans, service bureaus, or manual systems can offer.

The best way to determine whether or not accounting software makes sense for you, and, if so, which off-the-shelf packages you should consider, is to read multiproduct reviews of accounting products in personal computer magazines, seek out the experience of others with needs similar to yours, or work with an accounting consultant who has a thorough knowledge of PC-based automated accounting solutions—and of your particular needs.

MUSIC

APPLICATIONS
AND
ACTIVITIES:
GET WITH
THE
PROGRAM

55

The part of a personal computer that beeps when there's a problem, or bloops and buzzes when you destroy space aliens, can also produce musical notes. Most machines based on the IBM PC standard can play only one note at a time with their built-in sound hardware; other PCs—the Macintosh and Amiga, for example—are capable of playing full chords and multiple melodies. Some music applications turn the PC into a jukebox that plays a selection of tunes, such as Christmas carols. Other apps let you write your own music, in some cases by drawing notes on a musical staff on the screen. You can also find music tutorial applications that provide automated instruction in music theory, ear training, and other music-related pursuits.

If your ear tires of the computer's own sounds, you can probably add special hardware called a *sound board* that produces more notes at a time and finer-sounding instruments. Each sound board usually comes with its own musical applications that offer a selection of prepared sounds, allowing users to create new instruments or to write and edit compositions that the board will play.

Thanks to a music-industry standard called MIDI (the Musical Instrument Digital Interface), most electronic instruments can be connected. With a MIDI connection, fingering one keyboard can play the sounds of several instruments. Your personal computer can join the MIDI party when you install a hardware device called a MIDI interface board (some computers, such as the Atari ST, come standard with a MIDI interface). This allows you to use your PC as an instrument in an ensemble of electronic instruments.

MIDI is multifaceted. You can use it to record audio information such as when individual notes begin and end, along with other musical nuances such as loudness and pitch blending. Through MIDI, you can use musical applications that can record a performance from several electronic keyboards and drum machines and play back that sequence of notes through those instruments or others that are MIDI-smart. Such applications are called *sequencers* because they handle sequences of notes and other musical instructions.

Other MIDI apps are *notation programs* that experienced musicians who are also PC-savvy use to write complex musical scores and either play them immediately through MIDI instruments or print them out for live musicians to read. Some programs can even record live performances on a MIDI keyboard and turn them into printed music. Applications are available that allow users to tidy up wrong notes and make the notation clearer. Other applications, called *algorithmic composers*, create and play music on demand; the computer follows your broad instructions about the characteristics of the sounds (which turn out, at the computer's best, like "Space Music").

A MIDI-smart PC can help some electronic instruments maintain their sound libraries, and give you an easier way to create new sounds. Some MIDI instruments provide hundreds of ways to fine-tune each sound they generate. Other MIDI instruments, called *samplers*, record an actual sound (such as your speaking voice) and let the user edit it to sound at any pitch in any rhythm (H-H-H-Hello Max H-H-H-Headroom). Music applications let you use the computer's keyboard and screen to control a complicated instrument more comfortably than with the instrument's own tiny readout and cramped control panel.

Some MIDI instruments have no visible controls at all—these *sound modules* are designed to be played by a computer or another MIDI instrument's keyboard. Since the sound modules omit expensive controls (such as knobs and a keyboard), they can provide your PC with powerful sounds at a lower cost.

Music applications offer you great creative power—but may tempt you to bust your budget building up a bigger and better orchestra in your home.

MULTIMEDIA

APPLICATIONS
AND
ACTIVITIES:
GET WITH
THE
PROGRAM

57

Multimedia is exactly what the word suggests: mixed media. The concept of "mixing media" is not new; in fact, it's at least as ancient as classical Greek drama (remember the chorus?). Those "sound and light" shows so popular at big, outdoor tourist attractions like the Colosseum in Rome are multimedia productions. Any presentation involving more than one visual or audio element—a human narrator, a slide projector, and a tape recorder, for example—is a multimedia event.

What's new and interesting about multimedia is the increasingly important role personal computers are starting to play in creating and controlling multimedia productions.

The fact that such productions can be developed and controlled with PCs has led to an explosion of interest from companies and institutions that create multimedia productions (or more typically, hire experts to create them) to introduce new products or services to their sales staffs, distributors, or customers. Or as a training tool to introduce teachers to a new educational technique, for example, or inform new staffers of employee policies and benefits. Or even to promote a city, industrial park, or real estate development. The list of possible applications for multimedia is endless.

PC-based multimedia presentations are often relatively mobile and easy to set up. In addition, they can be designed to be *interactive*, allowing viewers to pick and choose the parts of the presentation they find most interesting.

Multimedia, while useful to a broad spectrum of individuals and enterprises, is often a fairly rarefied application requiring special hardware and software, as well as systems know-how and solid creative instincts. It is of particular interest to companies large enough to set up their own multimedia departments (or add this capability to in-house creative service departments) and to independent producers in the business of providing creative services to others. On the other hand, there's a strong trend toward easy-to-use multimedia programs that allow average users to create remarkably sophisticated presentations on their personal computers. These are proving increasingly popular with individuals, schools, small businesses, and anyone with a need to convey information or create interest in a product, service, or enterprise of any kind.

PROJECT MANAGEMENT

Your daughter has just revealed her not entirely unexpected betrothal. Fortunately, you're fond of her fella. Unfortunately, she wants a "Wedding of the Century"— and wants you to plan every last little detail. You have five months to pull everything together. Tick, tick, tick.

Quite unexpectedly, the academic committee said yes. Now there's no turning back; it's time to begin research on your doctoral thesis. The world, and your Ph.D. await. Tick, tick, tick.

You've complained for years about the decrepitude of the disgraceful ruin housing the TV station where you work. Congratulations: The station's moving to new quarters across town! Condolences: You get to manage the move. Tick, tick, tick.

In all these cases and a million others, project management software can help. These programs provide a framework for defining priorities, estimating time and resources needed, and measuring progress. Based on your input, they generate time lines and other graphic representations to help you clear your mind and stay on track. Still, for all the help they may offer in organizing big projects, these are not everyday programs. They tend to be quite specialized and difficult to use.

TRAINING SOFTWARE

APPLICATIONS
AND
ACTIVITIES:
GET WITH
THE
PROGRAM

59

Instructional programs are designed to teach who, what, when, why, and where. Training software aims to build skills, to teach how.

There are lots of off-the-shelf how-to programs available in many categories. In addition, companies and institutions with special training and orientation needs sometimes commission training programs for the exclusive use of their employees.

The most widely used training programs are those designed to introduce you to your personal computer and teach you how to use it. You can also find how-to training software covering computer languages (languages are software codes used to create applications), as well as certain brand-name applications, especially word processors, database management systems (see page 36), electronic spreadsheets (page 38), and desktop publishing applications (page 51).

If you've got all the PC stuff covered, how's your typing . . . er, keyboarding? There are several effective, surprisingly animated (literally), and even fun typing instructors available. A sampling of other categories: speed reading, music theory, weight loss, bartending programs, cooking programs, car maintenance programs, blackjack, and any number of other vocational skill builders and handyman helpers. See also: Instructional Programs, page 27.

STATISTICS

Statistical analysis plays a huge if largely hidden role in modern life. Insurance companies are rife with statisticians. So are government agencies, the natural and social sciences, marketing companies, weather bureaus, airlines, car makers, commodity traders. These "masters of the mean" are in the business of drawing a big picture from a pinhole view, among other things.

When Sincereal, Inc., for example, wants to know if its new product, Country Crunch, will fly, it doesn't ship boxes of the stuff to all the villes and burgs of the United States. This would be unacceptably expensive. Instead, sampling wizards identify a representative group to stand in for America ("Will it play in Peoria?"). Or if the group isn't representative, they use statistics to determine how the test group differs from the whole. The idea is to extrapolate from an infinitesimal sample whether the United States at large or some portion thereof wants anything to do with Country Crunch.

The tools of statisticians are sampling theory, probability, standard deviation, and increasingly the personal computer. Statistical analysis is a great application for PCs because it provides formulas and automates the computations. Some programs help set up the research as well. There are different kinds of statistical programs just as there are different kinds of statistical analysis. So if you need a program that handles curve fitting, crosstabs, and correlations, for example, be sure these capabilities are included.

COMPUTER-AIDED DESIGN (CAD)

APPLICATIONS
AND
ACTIVITIES:
GET WITH
THE
PROGRAM

61

Formerly, architects, engineers, drafters, and product designers spent many years learning how to put pencil to paper in order to translate raw ideas into plans that contractors and manufacturers could use to build houses, produce automobiles, or wire computer chips—in short, to make things.

Today, architects, engineers, drafters, and product designers still spend many years learning how to translate raw ideas into meaningful plans. But increasingly, they use PCs (or more powerful computers called *workstations*) and an application called computer-aided design, or CAD (rhymes with dad) rather than T-squares, triangles, and mechanical pencils.

CAD, of course, cannot turn bad architects and engineers into good ones, but like word processors, CAD can contribute to breathtaking gains in efficiency and accuracy. For example, a drafter can instantly change the design of 900 identical windows in a skyscraper plan by making the change in only one window and instructing the program to duplicate the alteration throughout. The ability to make such quick, large-scale alterations not only increases efficiency, it also contributes to creativity by making it easy to experiment.

Many CAD applications translate designs into 3-D representations. Some even allow you to rotate these models on screen to view your designs from different perspectives.

And, of course, you may print or plot what you create on the screen. Plotting requires a special printerlike hardware device called a . . . *plotter* (see page 100).

Most CAD programs, intended for use by specialists and professionals, are costly and complex. However, relatively inexpensive CAD applications are widely available, including several products targeted at users interested in remodeling rooms or designing their own houses and gardens.

DECISION SUPPORT

PC-based decision support software (DSS) is designed to do what the name implies: help make decisions—big, important decisions, mainly. A thriving mail-order company may use DSS, for example, to help it weigh the advantages and disadvantages of building a new distribution center. If the company decided to go ahead and build, it could use DSS to help choose from among several proposed sites.

While the uses of DSS are endless, this application's usefulness is limited: Decision support software cannot actually make decisions for you—only people can make decisions. DSS is designed to help you identify options; clarify your requirements, or "musts"; specify the pros and cons, or "arguments," associated with each option; and weigh the merits or deficiencies of each argument by assigning a relative value to it. You, of course, must identify the options, the pros and cons of each option, and the relative values. Typical programs provide fill-in-the-blank models for doing this, analyze your entries, and make a recommendation.

APPLICATION ENHANCERS (ADD-IN SOFTWARE)

Application enhancers are often called *add-in software* because you use them to extend the speed, capabilities, or ease of use of particular applications, especially word processors, databases, spreadsheets, and professional desktop publishers.

You can, for example, buy electronic *templates* for some spreadsheet programs. These are ready-made spreadsheet grids that contain built-in formulas for doing all kinds of things, from determining personal net worth to forecasting the break-even point for a real estate development.

APPLICATIONS
AND
ACTIVITIES:
GET WITH
THE
PROGRAM

63

HARDWARE AND SOFTWARE ENHANCERS (UTILITIES)

Utilities are software, but they're not applications in the normal sense. Instead, they're *enhancements*—small, usually inexpensive programs for making your system hardware or peripherals, e.g., printers, run faster, run better, do more things, or operate with greater ease of use.

There's a printer utility, for example, that allows you to print sideways, a very helpful capability, especially for printing wide spreadsheets.

Many users install "screen savers," utilities that automatically black out the image on your monitor during periods of inactivity, extending the life of the screen. The monitor reactivates automatically when you touch the keyboard or move the mouse, restoring the original image. You can also get a utility that blacks out the screen with the touch of a key, useful for hiding electronic games when the boss walks by.

Many PC users also own some kind of *file recovery program*, a utility that retrieves work or applications if they're mistakenly erased, a common PC mishap with electronic media. Other utilities are available for converting standard display type on the monitor to "big type" for those with weak vision, for electronically encoding work files to make them secure, and for tidying up the contents of a hard disk, to name a few uses.

Utilities are secondary considerations. You don't need to worry about them at the outset. Once you become more familiar with your PC and favored applications, you'll become aware of utility requirements and options as needs that arise and from word of mouth. As with applications and all aspects of PCs, don't assume that just because a utility or add-in program is available, it's worthwhile. Utilities are meant to be problem solvers. If there's no problem, chances are pretty good you don't need a solution.

MISCELLANY

APPLICATIONS
AND
ACTIVITIES:
GET WITH
THE
PROGRAM

65

Some wrongheaded teacher once told me that only lazy writers resort to that tired old category "Miscellaneous." I never accepted this hidebound point of view. Good thing, too, because many personal computer applications, like other aspects of life on earth, simply defy categorization. It would be impossible to list every tough-to-classify application available today, but the following mentions will give you an idea of their range. Incidentally, just because an application defies categorization doesn't mean it's offbeat or unworthy. Many sui generis (in a class by themselves) apps are indispensable to many users.

One of the most popular applications I know of for kids —I should say "for families" because this program provides an activity that parents can participate in—allows you to use your PC and a printer to print patterns for cutting, folding, gluing, and constructing paper models of cars, airplanes, castles, and all kinds of neat things. Kids love this program, especially as they can customize the patterns in many different ways. Is this a graphics program, an instructional program, or a game? It doesn't really matter; what counts is that the application is clever, interesting, inexpensive, and fun.

Many people neglect to write wills not because they're deluded about their own mortality but because they don't want to spend hundreds of dollars on attorney fees. Fortunately, there's a terrific little application available that generates Last Will and Testament templates and advice. This program is not a lawyer and it doesn't pretend to be one, but it also recognizes that lawyers are not essential to writing legally binding wills. This particular application has inspired similar programs for other consumer-oriented legal needs and requirements.

Many sophisticated database programs and some word processors include a capability for printing mailing labels. But you can also find stand-alone programs that specialize in automating this task, saving untold hours and expense.

Many people consider any conversation about the weather small talk. But there are those, including me, who find weather and weather forecasts endlessly fascinating. It turns out that there's an application available that downloads up-to-the-minute weather data via modem (communications hardware) from phone lines and prints current weather maps. This application also has obvious benefit as a teaching tool.

Need help being creative? How about trying something called an "idea generator," an application designed expressly to help users come up with ideas on any subject at any time.

The sampling above is only that, a sampling, and an extremely bare-bones one at that. If you're interested in knowing more about unclassifiable applications, pay a visit to any reasonably well-stocked software store or spend a few minutes paging through the ads of an ad-stuffed personal computer magazine, paying particular attention to the cataloglike direct-mail software ads or the classified ads in the back. You're almost certain to find all kinds of miscellaneous application software, some interesting, some completely irrelevant. The main point: If there's a shared need or interest, there's likely to be a personal computer application serving that need or interest.

THE REST OF THE APPLICATIONS STORY

APPLICATIONS
AND
ACTIVITIES:
GET WITH
THE
PROGRAM

67

Using applications is rarely just a matter of bringing one home, popping it into your floppy drive—and presto!—converting your PC to a specialized machine. There are, I'm obliged to report, other considerations. . . .

EASE OF USE

A simple shoot-'em-up arcade-style computer game is a vastly different creature from a complex multipurpose database management system. On the one hand, you could probably start the game up and play it within minutes of bringing it home—maybe without even bothering to look at the instructions. Mastering a complex database, on the other hand, would likely require many hours of training and weeks, months, or even years of experience.

You could say the game is a lot easier to use than the database, and you would be correct. So what? Boiling a hot dog is a lot easier than preparing *canard à la presse,* but who wants to eat hot dogs morning, noon, and night?

The point is—as you already know, because it's true about everything—you can't compare apples and oranges. Still, *ease of use* is a valid and important dimension of applications. Whatever they're designed to do, natural and responsive programs are better than cryptic and angst-inspiring ones.

But beware. Just because an application claims to be easy to use doesn't mean it is. Don't trust the label. Get confirmation through product demos, word of mouth, or published reviews. For more about these and other sources of product information, see page 133.

MANUALS (INSTRUCTION FOR USE)/ ON-SCREEN HELP/TUTORIALS

Off-the-shelf applications are all sold with some kind of operating instructions, or *documentation,* as it's frequently called. In simple applications (most games, many instructional programs) the instructions are often little more than a cheaply printed page or two. Complex applications, however, typically provide huge, daunting, positively monastic-looking *manuals,* sometimes spread over several volumes.

Manuals for major applications often come in two

parts: a *tutorial* and a *reference.* The tutorial portion consists of lessons designed to familiarize you with the application. The reference explains the full range of the program's commands and procedures. Complex applications with hundreds of commands and procedures come with correspondingly big reference sections that can't help but look intimidating, especially to newcomers. Things usually aren't as bad as they appear, however, for no one expects you to commit hundreds of commands to memory. Instead, chances are that once you master the application you'll use only twenty or twenty-five commands 98 percent of the time. As for the rest, you can look them up in the manual when you need them.

Many applications now provide built-in on-screen references as well as conventional ones in book form. These are called *on-screen help,* or sometimes, *context-sensitive help.* On-screen help allows you, while using the program, to call up "Help Screens" that attempt to explain operating procedures or answer technical questions while you're in the midst of using the program.

Like printed manuals, on-screen help can only do so much. It's simply impossible to anticipate every single problem or question users might have. If you're going to take on difficult applications (and there's no reason why you shouldn't), it helps to have access to a real person who knows more than you do or to supplement the manual with a well-organized, well-written book published independently by a company that specializes in computer titles. These books are designed to augment the manual or compensate for its shortcomings, which can be innumerable to the point of being overwhelming. Most major applications have inspired half-a-dozen or more associated reference or tutorial books. Spend a little time looking such books over before plopping down $20 or $30 or more on them, though, as they're not all geared to the same target audience, and quality can be woefully uneven. Many are no better than the original documentation.

Some applications, while they may be complex, are inherently easier to use than others. This is largely because they are cleverly designed to minimize the need for memorization of commands. Instead, commands and procedures are either intuitive (more-or-less obvious) or they can be revealed in *pulldown menus* (lists of commands) right on the screen. Believe me, intuitive, easy-to-use applications are much more desirable than balky ones. You're more likely to find the former if your PC is equipped to provide what's called a *graphical user inter-*

face or *GUI* (pronounced "gooey"). For more information about GUIs, see page 111.

WHAT YOU SEE IS WHAT YOU GET

There are two kinds of applications in the world. The first kind is called WYSIWYG (pronounced wizzy-wig), which may look like the name of a village in Wales but actually stands for What You See Is What You Get—as in what you see on the monitor is what you get when you print the document.

The second kind is best described with appropriate adjectives: remote, dunderheaded, and old-fashioned. Guess which one most users, newcomers and veterans alike, prefer.

To appreciate the difference, you really have to see it. But here's a small example. Let's say you're working on a non-WYSIWYG word processor and want to mark a sentence for italics. You enter the simple command, but instead of changing the sentence to italics on the monitor, your non-WYSIWYG program turns it dark blue. Later on, you want to mark a word for boldface. You enter the simple command, but instead of changing the word to boldface on the monitor, the program changes it to light blue. One paragraph down you want to underline a sentence. You enter the simple command, but instead of underlining it on the monitor, the word processor changes it to green.

When you print your document, you'll get real italics, boldface, and underlining on paper. In the meantime, you just have to remember what the *codes*—dark blue, light blue, and green—mean on the monitor. In any case, what you see definitely ain't what you get. Actually, this wouldn't be so difficult if all you had to remember were three codes. But non-WYSIWYG programs are loaded with obfuscating codes.

This is a frustrating way to have to work; you shouldn't be required to play guessing games on the job. Why not just make the document appear on the monitor as it will appear when you print it? Exactly.

In the early days of PCs, before hardware and software technology had a decade to evolve, cryptic codes to indicate italics and boldface and a zillion other qualities were standard in all kinds of applications. But today WYSIWYG has become the norm for many apps, especially word processing, graphics, form-making programs, and desktop publishing.

Still, make no assumptions. And even if a program declares 100 percent WYSIWYG! in screaming letters on the package, make sure it's true by asking for a demo.

COMPATIBILITY

When you walk into a software store, you'll notice that applications are separated into sections by type of personal computer: IBM, Macintosh, Apple II, and Amiga, for example. In addition, the IBM area may be subdivided into DOS, Windows, and OS/2 sections.

By-and-large if you own a Macintosh, you should assume that you can use *only* Macintosh-compatible applications, those specifically designed to run on Macintoshes. If you own an IBM personal computer (or an IBM-standard machine—one that works like an IBM) you should assume that you have to use IBM-compatible applications. And so forth.

Just as recording companies usually release new music in several formats—LP, cassette tape, and CD—applications publishers increasingly develop versions of an application for more than one kind of personal computer. So if you own a Mac, and something in the IBM section of the store catches your eye, don't linger longingly in the IBM section. Head for the Macintosh area and see if you find a version of the same product that's compatible with your Macintosh.

If you anticipate a need to share data or applications with an incompatible PC, products and strategies are available that, in some cases, get around the limits of compatibility. (To repeat: Never assume that this is possible.) For example, if you use an IBM-standard PC to write a proposal that needs to be amended by your partner, who uses a Macintosh, you could send your text to her via telephone lines (you would both need modems and communications software). She would then have the text on her floppy or hard disk just as if she had created it herself. This transfer would not preserve your formatting codes, however. Formatting codes are the commands you execute to double space lines, make words boldface, and so forth. Despite its limits, this approach, called an *unformatted data transfer*, is a very simple and therefore common solution to a persistent problem.

There are other options for transferring data between incompatible machines, and even for running incompatible applications. *Rich text format* transfers (RTFs), for example, allow different machines on the same network (a group of personal computers wired together) to send and receive text with formatting codes intact. The problem is, you need to be linked to a network to take advantage of this option. So-called *interoperable applications* are expressly designed to allow you to create files on one version of the application and transfer them to an otherwise incompatible machine. Some interoperable apps even allow you to exchange user-created programs—spreadsheet calculations, for example—between otherwise incompatible machines.

There are still other ways of dealing with inherent incompatibilities among different kinds of personal computers. Some computer hardware and software stores offer data-conversion services for a fee. Most other advanced solutions, however, require advance planning, compromises, investment in new hardware or software, or greater technical sophistication than most newcomers to personal computing possess. Still, they can link you to a larger world of applications and users. For more information, talk to a PC dealer, attend a user group meeting, or call on your personal PC guru.

The differences between Macs, IBM machines and compatibles, Apple IIs, and Amigas are explored and explained in "The Choices," page 117.

REQUIREMENTS

Every application comes with a set of minimum conditions that must be met before the application will run.
These *requirements* are always listed on the outside of
the box or package containing the application software.

Most personal computers meet the requirements of
most applications, so there's no problem. Sometimes,
though, users are surprised to discover that their system
lacks the necessities to run a particular application. To
avoid surprise: Know your system and always pay attention to the requirements listed on the box.

There are two kinds of requirements: hardware and
software. Hardware requirements concern internal components like enhancement boards (see page 80), hard
disks, input devices (some applications, for example, require a mouse), the monitor (a color application will not
display color on a monochrome monitor), and other parts
of the system. Software requirements almost always concern the operating system (all applications are operating
system-specific) and RAM capacity. RAM capacity is explained in How to Choose a Personal Computer, page
106.

The bottom line about application requirements
bears repeating: When you shop for applications, know
your system and always pay attention to the requirements listed on the box.

WARRANTIES/UPGRADES/FREE HELP

Personally, I'm the sort who usually throws warranty
cards into a kitchen drawer and forgets about them. At
least, I forget about them until my Friend-for-Life toaster
stops popping or the filament in my Forever light bulbs
burns out.

Now I know this probably isn't rational. But I also
know that mine is not an uncommon response.

In the first place, I can't stand the smarmy language
on warranty cards ("Congratulations! You've just made a
wise investment . . ."). Besides, the warranty usually
looks more like a market survey than a reliable guarantee.

Where did you purchase your Forever light bulbs?:
   A—Department store
   B—Hardware store
   C—By catalog
   D—Other

Questions like this always inspire the vestigial rebel in me to say, "It's none of your #@%*& business!"

In addition, I usually assume that if something actually does break, the hassle and cost of trying to get it fixed under warranty won't be worth the effort. Life's too short. So I take my chances . . . except when it comes to applications. Since you're reading my book in part to benefit from my experience, take my advice: When you buy a new application, fill out the registration card and send it in, even if you have to provide the stamp.

Sending in the registration is important because it entitles you to free or reduced price *upgrades* (improved versions) of the application as they're released. It may also authorize you to use a free telephone *help line*, if the software publisher offers one. Publisher-sponsored help lines provide technical and operational assistance.

New *versions*, or *releases*, as upgrades are also called, of an existing application are intended to do several things. For one, they attempt to keep the application current with changes in hardware and system software technology. Second, they typically contain new features based on feedback from users. And third, they correct problems, called *bugs*, in the previous version. On the one hand, bugs are usually minor glitches that, while irksome, do not compromise the application's overall performance. On the other hand, just as you can bleed to death from a thousand superficial cuts, a program shot through and through with bugs could be fatally flawed. Programs with an excessive number of bugs are said to be *buggy*.

TRANSFERRING WORK BETWEEN APPLICATIONS (EXPORTING/IMPORTING DATA)

Rare is the personal computer user who works with only one application. Experienced PC users, and even not-so-experienced ones, typically use several, sometimes many, apps. Or they work closely with others who use different applications. This being the case, PC users often need to transfer their work—text, numerical data, or graphics—from one application to another.

Imagine, for example, that you're writing a report with a word processor. The report cites figures you calculated with an electronic spreadsheet. Ideally, you would like to do more than merely cite the figures; you'd like to exhibit them graphically by converting the raw numbers to bar charts and placing these bar charts in your reports.

Your word processor does not make bar charts, so you're going to have to use a different program to do this. Fortunately, you've got a great little business graphics program that takes raw numbers and converts them, according to your instructions, to any of several kinds of comparative charts and graphs. So creating bar charts is no problem. But first you have to get your numerical data, the raw numbers you calculated with an electronic spreadsheet, into the graphics program. Then, after you use the graphics program to generate the charts and graphs you need, you have to get them into your textual report.

Fortunately, lots of applications are designed to allow this kind of transfer of work. But not all do, so you cannot —must not—make any assumptions about this capability. If you're new to PCs and think you may have a need to move data around between applications, be sure the apps you buy allow this. Many programs list import/export capabilities on the box. A graphics program, for example, will advertise the fact that it's compatible with a leading electronic spreadsheet application or with specified word processors.

If in doubt, as always, get a demonstration, either from a friend or colleague or from a software store.

COPYING APPLICATIONS

We are copy-crazy people. Copy machines are everywhere, of course, but they're the least of it. We also copy music, telephone calls, and television shows. Routinely. Without a second thought.

Personal computers are a part of this tradition. You can use a PC to copy applications (and data files) easily and instantly. This is good, for there are lots of reasons to make copies with the PC.

One is to make *backups*, extra copies of applications that serve as a form of software insurance should something happen to the originals. If you have more than one personal computer—one at home and one at the office, for example—you may also have a legitimate need for multiple copies of an application.

It is illegal to copy most applications, however, in order to pass them out to friends, or worse, to sell them. True, copying for these purposes is as easy as smiling. And yes, copying is virtually undetectable. It is also no different than shoplifting. Some programs are *copy-protected*, which means that the publisher has built an elec-

APPLICATIONS
AND
ACTIVITIES:
GET WITH
THE
PROGRAM

75

tronic lock into the software limiting the number of times you can make copies. Copy protection is a major consumer issue because you may have legitimate reasons for making more copies of the application than the copy-protection scheme allows. Applications that are copy-protected say so on the package.

COMPUTER LANGUAGES

Every novel, every written instruction, every dictionary, and every encyclopedia have at least one thing in common: They could not exist, they could not convey meaning without language. The same is true of computer applications, except that applications are derived from computer language rather than from familiar human language.

Like human language, computer language (often called *programming language*) is a set of formal notation governed by rules and standards. When arranged expertly, the notation provides meaningful instructions to the computer, instructions we call applications. When you use an application, you are actually selecting and manipulating the electronic instructions devised by a programmer who wrote them in a computer language.

There are many programming languages, including many special-purpose ones. The most familiar computer languages in the personal computer universe are assembly language, C (that's its full name), COBOL (common business-oriented language), FORTRAN (formula translator), and Pascal, named for the seventeenth-century French inventor. These are all largely the province of very advanced PC users and professional application developers.

The most popular—because it is versatile and relatively accessible—computer language among PC users is called BASIC, an acronym for Beginners All-purpose Symbolic Instruction Code. Still, only a small minority of PC users bother to learn about BASIC. Those who do use it to modify their commercial applications or even create their own.

If you think you would be interested in exploring computer language, BASIC is probably a good place to begin. There are lots of introductory books on BASIC (and other computer languages). Classes in BASIC and other languages are commonly offered through local colleges, hardware and software stores, and seminars.

4

HARNESSING HARDWARE: GET A GRIP

There is only one good, knowledge, and one evil, ignorance.
—SOCRATES

ABOUT THIS SECTION

So far in this book, I've emphasized software, especially application software. Applications earn special attention because they take charge; they give identity and meaning to hardware that would otherwise be a good-for-nothing assortment of metal and plastic. So three cheers for applications: Glorious applications! Triumphant applications! Empyrean applications!

Of course, applications aren't the only kind of software; they're just the most conspicuous and, as far as most PC users are concerned, the most interesting kind. There's also system software, and several kinds of "deep brain" software, all of which, to give them their due, are just as vital as applications.

Without system software and applications, PC hardware is nothing but post-Cambrian carapaces stuffed with primitive moving parts and electrical connectors—latter-day smoke and mirrors. The central processing unit or CPU, the so-called brain of the system, is "a brain without a clue," worse than helpless, worse even than useless. The shocking truth: Without software, the CPU is pointless.

Just the same . . . what's a mind without a brain? Or body? It's ghastly, that's what. It's unthinkable. The late Anne Sexton in her poem, "The Earth," got it just about right. She wrote:

God owns heaven . . . but he envies the bodies, he who has no
    body.

Well, software—glorious, triumphant, empyrean software—also envies "the bodies," that is, the hardware. Because without hardware, applications and other software are helpless, useless . . . pointless. It's the old yin-yang dichotomy. You know: Plant and animal. Male and female. Good and evil. Mind and matter. Software and hardware.

This section is about the personal computer bodies: tactile, textural, solid, graspable, essential hardware.

Hardware comes in many varieties. Some kinds of hardware are the PC equivalent of vital organs. Collectively these are called core, or system hardware. Everything else—printers, modems, plotters, scanners—is called peripheral hardware or peripheral devices.

SYSTEM HARDWARE

The basic, stripped down, no-frills PC system has four parts:

The unimposing computer itself is called a central processing unit, CPU for short.

A monitor is the part of the PC that looks like a television set. *Video display terminal (VDT)* is another common name for the monitor, and some diehard language bashers even cling to the horrible old appellation, *cathode ray tube (CRT)*. Please don't be one of them. (Besides, CRT refers to only one kind of monitor.)

PCs use primarily two kinds of software storage media: portable floppy disks (you can remove them and carry them around) and unportable fixed hard disks. The devices for electronically retrieving stored software are called floppy disk drives and hard disk drives.

One or more input devices are used to give outside (human) instructions to the PC. There are quite a few different kinds of input devices, but only one, the keyboard, is universal. The computer mouse is also fast becoming a standard desktop partner to the keyboard.

CENTRAL PROCESSING UNIT

CPUs aren't very interesting to look at. In fact, they're 100 percent utilitarian-looking, bland, and boring. They definitely do not stand out in a crowd. Breadboxes are more exciting. Kitchen sinks are more visibly dynamic. Flashlights have winning personalities by comparison.

But then—cliché alert!—Beauty is old skin deep . . . You shouldn't judge a PC by its cover . . . It's what's inside that counts.

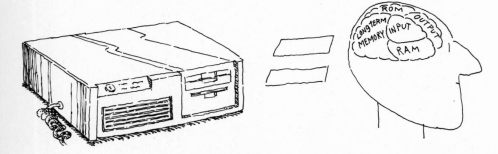

True enough. The part of the CPU that you can see is merely the case. All the dynamic stuff is inside the box.

The importance of the CPU so outweighs everything else that to veteran PC users the terms *computer* and *CPU* are completely interchangeable; the CPU *is* the computer. It's where the processing takes place. It is, in short, the brain of the system.

The CPU is usually the most expensive part of the system. And the most mysterious, in part because there's not much visible activity in there. A CPU is mainly a place for storing software and for routing electric impulses—electronic instructions and information.

Fortunately, you don't have to penetrate the mystery of what's going on inside the CPU in order to use it. Just as most television viewers would never think of poking around inside their TVs when the picture goes bad, most PC users never unscrew the back of their CPUs.

You can, however, customize a PC by adding or removing certain components inside the box (or having them added or removed by a technician, which is what most people do). Therefore, it's a good idea to know what's inside or has the potential to fit inside, at least roughly, even if you never expect to explore the CPU yourself.

MOTHER BOARD The *mother board*—also called a *system board*—is the Big Mama of the CPU (there is no Big Daddy). It's called a mother board mainly because there are "daughter boards" attached to it. (The role of daughter boards in the CPU is described in "Enhancement Boards," page 80.)

The mother board contains the *microprocessor*, the "heart of the brain," to coin a phrase—the master controller. This is an *integrated circuit chip*—a dense network of microscopic electrical pathways etched in highly refined sand, or *silicon*. The microprocessor is responsible for the basic elements of computer processing: arithmetic, logic, and control.

Some PC mother boards come with special-purpose performance boosters called *coprocessors* (which may also be added to the board later). These are integrated circuit chips designed to enhance performance in a given area, mathematical processing, for example, or graphic imaging on the monitor. Coprocessors work only with applications designed to take advantage of them, but when everything is in synch, these little chips can accelerate processing speed tremendously. They're certainly not necessary, however, for routine personal computing.

In addition to the microprocessor, the mother
board provides a home for the CPU's *RAM chips.*
RAM stands for *random access memory*, but I prefer
to call it "short-term memory." RAM chips are storage cells for short-term memory.

Personal computers use short-term memory in
much the same way you and I do. When you share a
recollection—the recollection of an enchanted childhood birthday, let's say—with a friend, you're really
"downloading" the images, tastes, smells, sounds, and
feelings of that special day from your long-term memory to your short-term memory. In other words, you're
bringing the stored sensations to the active, in-the-mo-
ment forefront of your consciousness. When you're
finished describing your recollection, it sifts out of
your active memory, but remains in your long-term
memory.

Of course, you do this without thinking. It's routine. It's much the same with PCs. You can't use system software, applications, or data files a long as
they're only in long-term memory (stored on a floppy
disk or hard disk). You have to bring the apps or data
forward to short-term memory, the RAM: Hence, the
RAM chips come into play. The process for doing this
—for "calling up" an application or data—in a PC is
controlled by you, the user, executing simple, almost
automatic commands.

ENHANCEMENT BOARDS *Expansion slots* are spaces inside
the CPU reserved for *expansion boards* (also called *enhancement boards, daughter boards, plug-in boards,
adapter boards, add-in boards, option boards,* and
planar boards or expansion *cards,* enhancement cards,
and so on, depending on who's doing the talking). I'll
stick to enhancement board since that best describes
the function of these components, which is . . . to enhance, or even customize, your PC.

As crammed as the mother board is with chips
and plugs and circuitry, it can't possibly do everything
that every possible user might like it to do. To put it
in computerese, the mother board cannot *support*
every capability imaginable, including some you might
like to have in your PC.

That's why most PCs are designed to allow you to
enhance or customize your machine by snapping special-purpose enhancement boards into the expansion
slots. These are controlled by the mother board, to

which they connect, but they do things the mother board cannot do on its own.

Enhancement boards can add color capability or graphics or animation or sound—or improved sound—capabilities to a personal computer. They can speed up complex calculations and statistical analysis. You can even get hard disks and modems (the hardware that allows you to send and receive data over telephone lines) on enhancement boards. They also can add more RAM, short-term memory, than can fit on the mother board itself.

Sometimes you need more than a new board in order to make an enhancement to your PC. A color display enhancement board, for example, won't give you color displays if you have a monochrome (single-color) monitor.

In some personal computers, the manufacturer commandeers several expansion slots for boards—a video display adapter or floppy disk controller, for example—that provide essential services. So be aware that even though a CPU may be advertised as having five expansion slots, in reality, the slots may not all be available to use as you choose.

HARD DISKS/FLOPPY DISKS PCs need someplace to store applications, data, and system software when they're not in use, which is most of the time. PCs also need a way to fetch selected software from storage (as instructed by the user) and place it in RAM, the computer's short-term memory. You've got to place the software in RAM in order to be able to use it.

There are primarily two kinds of software storage places or *media:* floppy disks and hard disks. The two don't look anything alike. The floppy is compact, light, and very portable. You can store an application or a document on the floppy and carry it from one PC to another or even put it in a cardboard envelope and mail it to someone. Most hard disks, including internal hard disks and the external model shown, are not designed for portability.

The long-term storage media—the floppy and the hard disk—are passive; they don't *do* anything. In order to activate software stored in long-term memory, you must instruct the machine to fetch it and place it in RAM, short-term memory. (The machine doesn't actually remove the software from long-term memory; it places a copy of that information in RAM.)

The devices used to retrieve software from floppy disks and hard disks are called floppy disk drives and hard disk drives and disk drive controller boards.

Almost all CPUs come with one or two floppy drives in the front of the CPU. All you can see of them are the slots for inserting the floppy disk. Hard disks are optional, but most people who use PCs prefer to have a hard disk drive as well as one or two floppy drives.

Here's why. Floppy drives are like closets, hard disks are like warehouses full of movable partitions. They offer more room for storing system software, data, and applications and more flexibility in organizing them. Plus, with a hard disk, you don't have to bother slipping diskettes in and out of the floppy drive every time you want to start up the machine, change applications, or call up a data file. This is a major convenience. What's more, applications stored on the hard disk usually run faster. Anything that speeds up the system is appreciated. And finally, having both a hard disk drive and at least one floppy makes it easy to back up your work. *Backups* are duplicates of data or applications, a form of insurance against unexpected erasure of software.

Hard disks come in increments of 10 megabytes. (One megabyte equals about one million bytes, the equivalent of 700 pages of written text. For a more complete explanation of bytes, see "binary code," page 160.) Because long-term memory is fairly inexpensive these days, most users opt for hard disks with a capacity of between 20 and 50 megabytes, which is plenty as far as 95 percent of all users are concerned. The more megabytes of storage capacity, the more the hard disk costs, naturally.

Floppy disks come in two sizes: 5¼ inch and 3½ inch. Some personal computers use only 5¼-inch diskettes; some use only 3½-inch diskettes, and some can use either or both, but only if they're equipped with compatible—same size—floppy drives (you can't use a 3½-inch diskette if you have only a 5¼-inch floppy drive, and vice versa).

Three-and-a-half-inch diskettes are popular because they're more compact than the alternative. In addition, as they're enclosed in hard plastic, they're less subject to damage than 5¼-inch diskettes, which are flexible and which expose more of the magnetic storage medium. (The word "floppy," incidentally, refers to the flimsy plastic disk inside the plastic case.)

All floppy disks require some minor obeisance to the god of Preventive Care. Another floppy disk consideration everyone should be aware of is *density;* see page 155. For more information on diskette do's and don'ts see page 150.

POWER SUPPLY The CPU also contains a *power supply,* which converts household current to the form used by the PC. Most power supplies contain *surge protectors,* providing rudimentary protection to the CPU from electrical surges. A fan cools the power supply unit when the machine is on; it's the source of the whirring sound made by the activated CPU.

That completes the survey of a typical central processing unit, but not of system hardware. Descriptions of additional long-term memory storage devices, monitors, and input devices follow.

ADDITIONAL LONG-TERM MEMORY DEVICES

A hard disk drive and one or two floppy disk drives are de rigeur as far as most PC users are concerned. Some people, however, especially those whose livelihoods depend on their PCs (and the data they create with their PCs every day), augment their hard and floppy disk drives with an additional long-term memory device.

There are really only two reasons for augmenting the hard disk and floppies: to gain extra storage capacity and/or to make data more secure by storing work in three places instead of two (the hard disk and on floppies).

I have a friend, for example, who's a graphic designer. He and his partner and their staff work all day on Macintoshes. They're always in deadline panic. To lose a day's work would be disastrous. So they store everything on floppy disk and on *removable cartridges* (akin to audio-tape cassettes) as well as on the hard disk.

These handy units are compact and portable, providing extra insurance against data loss. The other option is *tape drives,* heavy duty, industrial-strength storage devices more suitable for larger companies that generate huge amounts of data on PCs every day than for individual PC users. Both forms of software storage require special recording devices. Companies that use tape drives often employ special *data compression* techniques to squeeze even more information into the long-term storage space available.

MONITORS

"Want some ketchup?" the ancient, henna-haired waitress in New York's old Penn Garden Hotel asked abruptly as she plopped my cheeseburger down on the counter. Before I could form an answer, she reached for a bottle of Heinz 57 Varieties, set it under my nose, and declared rhetorically (but emphatically), "Whatsa burga widout ketchup?"

The same question applies in slightly modified form here: *Whatsa PC without a monitor?*

Monitors are rightly considered system hardware because they're anything but peripheral. They make applications and your own keyboard-tapping (or mouse-manipulating) input visible, something usable, in short, something . . . human.

Actually, the monitor doesn't do the converting. In most machines, that's the job of the *display adapter*, which usually takes the form of an enhancement board —it snaps into one of the expansion slots inside the CPU. The display adapter and monitor work together to recast applications and data into something the monitor can use —and that we can see, hallelujah!

All monitors are not alike. Broadly, there are three considerations when choosing a monitor: screen size, resolution, and color. Cost is also, as always, a factor.

Screen size in PC monitors is measured the same way it's measured in televisions: diagonally. The advantage of big screens is that they display more data simultaneously. They may also improve resolution (sharpness of image). Big screens are especially useful for graphics applications and for desktop publishing, as they allow you to view the equivalent of one entire printed page of work. The disadvantage of big screens is that they take up more space and cost more. As for resolution: Just as clarity is preferable to befuddlement, higher resolution—sharper, more detailed video text images—is better than lower resolution.

Most people prefer color monitors to monochrome. With the right enhancement board, some monitors are capable of displaying millions of colors. Most people have little need for such a vast palette. "Monochrome," incidentally, does not necessarily mean black and white; it simply means single color, usually black and white, black and green, or black and amber. As a rule, monochrome monitors offer better resolution than color monitors; for this reason, users whose applications require especially high resolution often favor monochrome monitors.

KEYBOARD AND MOUSE

You've got to have a way to tell your computer what to do, to instruct it, to give it commands. When you want to use an application to change the PC to a specialized machine, you can't just say "abracadabra." And once you've converted the PC, you need some mechanism, method, or means to manipulate the application. You need, in short, an *input device.*

The keyboard and mouse are the primary input devices used to activate and manipulate applications and create, store, organize, and retrieve data—to do, in other words, a thousand and one (at least) different things.

If you've never examined one, personal computer keyboards may look strange at first glance, but upon closer inspection, they're not so exotic.

A typical personal computer keyboard. (Photo courtesy of Northgate Computer Systems, Inc.)

The letter, number, and punctuation/symbol keys—the *alphanumeric keys,* as they're called—are arranged in the same way as on regular typewriters. They include a backspace key, a space bar, a shift and tab key, and a good old carriage return, usually called simply *return key* or *enter key.*

The numbered keys (F1, F2, etc.) across the top of some keyboards are *function keys*. Their purpose is to allow you to execute commands in applications. Applications use function keys in different ways. For example, a word processor may reserve the F3 key for its "delete word" command. In contrast, a graphics application might assign its "zoom" command (enlarge image) to the F3 key. PC keyboards lacking function keys offer alternatives for executing commands.

The *numeric keypad* on the right side of the keyboard works as a calculator. The *arrow keys*, usually called *cursor keys*, are for moving the on-screen pointer. Generally, you can view the equivalent of only one page of text or other data on the monitor at one time. The page up and page down keys allow you to move around long documents quickly with the simple push of a specialized key.

Virtually every application contains dozens, even hundreds, of commands, many more commands than there are keys on a keyboard. Since there aren't enough keys for every command, applications require combinations of keystrokes for most commands.

If I want to delete a line of text in one word processor, for example, I hold down the *alternative key* (labeled *Alt*) and while holding it, strike the F5 (function key 5). If I want to make the line reappear, I hit the F3 key while holding down the Alt key. This illustrates the main purpose of the Alt key: to create more combinations of keystrokes.

Ditto the *control key* (labeled *Ctrl*). Keystroke combinations are not limited to the Ctrl key, Alt key, and function keys, however.

One way to remember what keys and keystroke combinations execute what commands is to place an application-specific *template* temporarily (for the length of the work session) over your keyboard. Templates are available for many applications. You should be able to find a selection of templates in software stores or bookstores with computer book sections. In addition, some applications are sold with keyboard templates. Whether you get a template with applications at the time of purchase or buy them separately, they can come in very handy, sparing you the tedious, time-consuming necessity of looking up commands and procedures you haven't yet committed to memory.

If you don't like the keyboard that comes with your personal computer, you can likely replace it with any of several alternative models. The main reasons people replace their keyboards, which are relatively inexpensive, are because their original keyboard lacks function keys, or because they want more function keys or they want the function keys in a different place. Sometimes PC users replace keyboards simply because they want a longer cord or because they don't like the feel and feedback of their own keyboard. (Some people like the keys to click when they strike them; others—especially users who spend a lot of time on the phone while they work—prefer silence.)

The keyboard traces its beginnings to the late nineteenth century; the mouse is a relatively recent innovation. It used to be—until Apple introduced the Macintosh in 1985—that the mouse was considered a strange alternate input device. Well, a lot of things used to be.

Not that mice replace keyboards. They don't; instead, they augment them. You cannot generate text with a mouse, at least not if you value your time. However, most PC users who spend a lot of time working with graphics or desktop publishing applications cannot imagine working without a mouse.

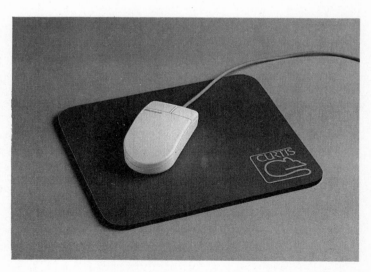

A computer mouse at rest on a mouse pad. Like a keyboard, this input device is used to give commands to applications and to create data. It got its name because it's about the same size as a mouse, it's mobile, and presumably the cord looks like a naked tail. (Photo courtesy of Curtis Manufacturing Company, Inc.)

Most mice are surprisingly simple mechanical devices with a ball protruding partway through a hole in the belly. By moving the mouse on a mousepad, you force the ball to turn. The ball's movement is tracked by sensors inside the mouse case and conveyed by a thin wire —the tail—to the CPU and monitor, where it controls the movement of the on-screen pointer.

Newer electronic mouse models are also available. You can also opt for something called a *track ball*, in which the motion ball protrudes through the keyboard, or is self-contained in a separate unit, allowing you to roll it with the palm of your hand or tips of your fingers.

A trackball is an "alternative input device," a cousin to the keyboard and computer mouse. It works like a mouse except that instead of moving a device over a flat surface, you move the exposed ball with the palm of your hand. (Photo courtesy of Logitech.)

Some personal computers, notably Macintoshes, come with a mouse as standard equipment. Others leave it up to you to decide for yourself if you want to buy a mouse. In some PCs, installing a mouse is not simply a matter of plugging it in, clicking, and pointing; you also have to install corresponding software called a *mouse driver*.

OTHER INPUT DEVICES

The keyboard and, increasingly, the mouse are standard input devices. But there are other special-purpose options.

JOYSTICKS *Joysticks* are sturdy, multidirectional, and ultraresponsive control devices used mainly for playing computer arcade and action games.

Joysticks like the one shown are specialized input devices used mainly to control computer games. (Photo courtesy of Advanced Gravis Computer Technology, Ltd.)

LIGHT PENS AND TOUCH SCREENS *Light pens* are electronic pointers employed mainly for drawing or editing graphics directly on the screen as if the screen were a piece of paper. Light pens sound nifty, but in reality, most users find holding the pen up to the screen tiring and therefore inefficient.

Touch screens are like light pens except you do the pointing with your . . . finger! They're mainly used on PCs set up to disgorge public information. ("Are you interested in restaurants, museums, shopping, historical sites? Please choose one by touching the screen.")

SCANNERS *Scanners* are special input devices that allow you to transfer photographs, graphic images, or text from magazines, newspapers, glossy photographs, brochures, and other printed sources to the PC. The scanner converts the image to a form that can be manipulated by applications and stored in long-term memory.

Why would anyone want to do this? Let's say you're using a desktop publishing program to design a newsletter for your civic association. You want to include photographs of the new club officers in the newsletter. How do you get images from the photos into the newsletter? With a scanner—via the PC.

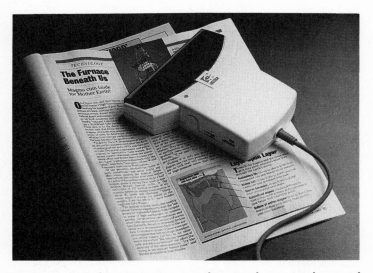

Scanners are used to "import" text and images from printed material to the PC. Once they are in the PC, you can alter them or combine them with other text or images in reports, newsletters, and other documents you create using a word processor, a desktop publishing program, or graphics applications. (Photo courtesy of Logitech.)

Over the last few years scanners have tumbled in price and soared in reliability. There are basically two kinds: *desktop scanners* and *hand-held scanners*, the less expensive alternative.

OPTICAL CHARACTER READERS Imagine that you are compiling a booklet of reminiscences for your parents' fiftieth wedding anniversary. You've invited 200 family members, friends, neighbors, and colleagues to contribute stories and anecdotes. You receive 140 typed replies, some of them quite long. You have a personal computer and a trusty word processing program, but you're nonetheless faced with the daunting task of retyping all the submissions in order to get them into the system so that you can edit them with the word processor and use a desktop publishing or graphics program to design the booklet.

OCRs, optical character readers, working in tandem with OCR software, provide an alternative. These devices are specialized scanners that recognize letter shapes. They work by scanning (electronically filming) printed text and converting it electronically to digital data—software. The result is much the same as if you had actually retyped (or rekeyed) the text yourself, except that you save hours, maybe days, of work.

Currently, most OCRs are specialized and expensive, usually limited to work environments—insurance companies, law offices, government agencies—where there's a high volume of printed matter to convert to software. The push is on, however, to make OCR technology more available to small businesses and individuals. Already, some image scanners, described above, are capable of "reading" and converting text. If you think you have a need for this capability, you should investigate image and text scanners as well as more expensive high-volume OCR technology.

VOICE INPUT   One of the reasonable goals of some inventors is to create practical devices for executing commands and inputting data to the PC by voice instead of by tapping a keyboard or rolling a mouse over a flat surface. *Voice input,* as it's called, gets a lot of attention in the mainstream media, but practically speaking, it's still a technology of the future.

PERIPHERAL HARDWARE

The CPU, disk drives, input devices, and monitor—system hardware—are a personal computer's vital organs. *Peripheral devices*, as they're usually called, are not essential, at least not in the same as-I-live-and-breathe sort of way, but that doesn't mean they're frivolous, or even optional. Someone whose work, for example, is heavily dependent on PC communications would be hard put to do without a peripheral device—the modem—that makes such communications possible.

What follows are descriptions of the most common categories of personal computer peripheral hardware.

PRINTERS

The single most important species of peripheral hardware is the *printer*. A printer is not vital, perhaps, but then neither is the human voice. Printed pages are to the PC what the voice is to humans—the principal form of expression. I don't know one person, not a single one, who owns or uses a PC who doesn't have, or have nearby access to, a printer.

There are basically three categories of printers for the PC: *dot matrix*, *laser*, and everything else. These are described starting on page 96.

PRINTER BASICS, BACKGROUNDS, AND ADVICE

The printer market is deep and wide, but not unfathomable. The main considerations when shopping for a printer are print quality, printing speed, ease of use, noise, adaptability, and, as always, cost. These and other considerations are discussed below.

If you haven't spent much time around personal computers, you might think of PC printers as automated versions of typewriters. But typewriters are text machines only. Most PC printers can, if coupled with the right software, generate both text and graphics, including charts, tables, illustrations, logos, maps, diagrams, and other images. With a scanner (see page 90) you can even print photographs.

PRINT QUALITY (RESOLUTION) The printed pages (or *output*) generated by many early personal computer printers looked more like connect-the-dot children's puzzles than what you're used to thinking of as printing on paper. Today, most printers do much better than that, and the best rival professional typesetting.

Print quality is usually measured in *dots per inch (DPI)*. The higher the DPI, the better the resolution. Six hundred DPI is superior for a PC printer; it's also exceedingly rare. DPIs of 400 and below are the norm. Not surprisingly, high-resolution printers generally cost more than lower-resolution models.

PRINTING SPEED Some printers are ponderously slow; others zip right along. The measure of a printer's speed is *pages per minute (PPM)* or *characters per second (CPS)*. Most printers cruise at somewhere between four and twenty-two pages per minute. If you or your business expect to do a lot of high-volume printing, speed will definitely be an issue. If not, it probably doesn't make sense to pay extra for a high-speed printer.

Some printers, especially dot matrix models, allow you to adjust printing speed. More accurately, they allow you to flip a switch to make a trade-off: faster printing, but lower-quality output. This option can be surprisingly useful because there are many times when print quality is not particularly important, but speed is.

Imagine, for example, that you have to write (using a word processor, of course) a fifty-page report. Upon finishing the first draft, you need to print it and pass it around to colleagues for written comments. Since this is the first of several working drafts rather than a final copy, you're more interested in getting the thing printed and circulated than in how the printing looks. So you switch your printer to fast-printing *draft mode*. Later, when you're ready to print the final version, you can switch the printer to its *quality mode*. The job will take longer this time, but that's the price of making the final copy look slick and professional.

EASE OF USE PC printers all come with control panels on the front. Sometimes these are nothing more than a couple or three twinkling little lights *(LEDs* they're called, for *light-emitting diodes)* to indicate if the machine is on or off, inform you that you're out of paper, or something equally benign.

The control panels can be more elaborate, however, displaying actual operating messages or providing buttons and switches that allow you to exercise various options (faster printing or special typefaces, for example). Some printer control panels, however, are sadistic experiments in consumer torture, designed to probe the endurance limits of bipeds. If the printer is designed with Tellurians (earthlings) in mind, the control panels will illuminate rather than mystify. Control panels, in other words, shouldn't require a whole lot of training to comprehend or ... control. Check this out before signing on the dotted line.

In addition, the rest of the printer should be easy to use. If you have to bend your fingers in painful new ways to load or adjust paper, for example, walk on by.

NOISE   If you're sensitive to noise and plan to use your printer next to your desk for long print runs, stop, look, and listen, before buying. Most printers specify their noise level in decibels. If noise is an issue with you, though, don't trust the rating; request an audition. Generally impact printers—dot matrix models, for example—are quite noisy whereas other printer technologies are much quieter.

LABELS/ENVELOPES/OVERSIZED PAPER   If you anticipate using your printer to print labels, envelopes, or oversized paper, be sure to confirm these capabilities with a demonstration before you bring the printer home or to the office.

COST   It should come as no surprise that a fast, quiet, reliable printer with output that looks professionally typeset is likely to cost more than a slow, noisy, tetchy printer. As with most things, you more or less get what you pay for. Still, with hundreds of products on the market, it's easy to become confused about the relative value of trade-offs involved (fast/slow, noisy/quiet, high-quality print/chicken scratches, etc.). A little research and comparison shopping can save you from getting less than you pay for. Useful (lucid, sensible, reliable) information about specific printers, based on independent comparative product testing, is widely available from personal computer magazines, many of which feature printer reviews regularly. Some periodicals also publish annual "roundups," collective reviews that not only compare and contrast the features and performance of dozens of printers but also include primers and recommendations based on partic-ular needs.

COLOR PC printers used to be like Model T Fords: You could print in any color as long as it was black. (Ac-tually, you could change to another single color by changing the ribbon cartridge, but this isn't the same as "color printing.")

Today, color printers are widely available, but monochrome (single-color) models overwhelmingly outsell them, mainly, no doubt, because most people are interested in printing text, and black text on white paper is an ancient convention. Just ask Gutenberg.

Besides, color printers that produce high-quality color pages are astronomically expensive, $10,000 and up. Without a doubt, the price will come down, but even at five digits, these high-end color printers make sense for certain professional applications—magazine publishing, for example—if not for most small busi-nesses, independent professionals, and home users. More primitive—much more primitive—color printers start at around $1000.

OTHER PRINTER CONSIDERATIONS Availability of on-site service may be important, especially if your work is heavily printer-dependent. Likewise, the size of the printer can be an issue if desk or office space is limited or if you need to haul the printer around with you.

SHARING A PRINTER Many offices, small businesses, and corporate departments (or floors in high-rise buildings) share printers and other peripheral devices by wiring several—or many—users to a single printer. This helps justify investment in faster, more expensive printers capable of generating high-quality output.

The disadvantage of sharing a printer is that work can back up (print orders are executed on a first-come, first-serve basis). On some systems, you may have to wait until your print job is finished before you regain the use of your computer. This sounds like a minor inconvenience, but it can be quite annoying if you do a lot of printing ("hurry up and wait"). Also, since the printer may be across the room or even in another room, the privacy of printed documents may be sacri-ficed. Like copy machines, however, shared printers often make good sense.

GOING WITHOUT A PRINTER Many cities, including smaller cities, have storefront desktop publishing businesses where you may pay (usually by the page) to use a PC printer. Normally, printers are available only for IBM, IBM-compatible, and Macintosh applications. Most PC users who take advantage of these services have their own printers; they use pay printers only to generate higher-quality or color pages.

TYPES OF PRINTERS

In the early days of the PC, most printers were jury-rigged typewriters. This approach to PC printing is still available, but then, so are washboards. During the early 1980s, impressive little workhorses known as *dot matrix printers* were favored by most PC users. In mid-decade, *laser printers* started earning high marks for the quality of their output. But lasers were very expensive, reserved at first for design and publishing concerns or companies that could justify spending lots of money for good-looking homegrown print.

Inevitably, the price of laser printers tumbled. Today, low-end laser models cost no more than high-end dot matrix printers. Dot matrix printers are still popular, though, because in the main, they're compact and lightweight but durable, simple but adaptable, and at the low end, quite inexpensive. They also cost less per page because dot matrix cartridges are much cheaper than toner, the raw ingredient of laser printing.

New PC printer technologies have begun to infiltrate the PC user community. Inkjet printers, models that actually spray ink on the page in a very controlled way to form characters and images, are also competing with dot matrix printers. But most other printer technologies are expensive, untested in a mass market, or reserved for special needs. No doubt, as these are perfected and prices drop, some will attract wide followings. For the present, dot matrix and laser printers deservedly remain the overwhelming favorites of most PC users.

DOT MATRIX PRINTERS If you place a sheet of carbon paper ink-side down on a sheet of plain paper and then tap the back of the carbon with a toothpick, the impact will transfer ink from the carbon to the plain paper, forming a single dot. Simple enough.

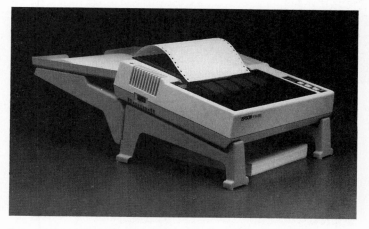

Dot matrix printers are noisy but versatile, efficient, reliable, and inexpensive. Most use perforated track paper. After a print job, you have to remove the perforated margins and tear off the individual sheets. Printer shown is an Epson FX-25. (Photo courtesy of Curtis Manufacturing Company, Inc.)

This is exactly how dot matrix printers work—except that they use up to twenty-four metal pins and an inked ribbon rather than a toothpick and carbon paper. Such impact printing resembles that of the common typewriter . . . with one critical difference. A typewriter key can print only the one or two characters embossed on the tip of it. A single set of pins in a dot matrix printer (receiving instructions from a software application) can print anything—lines, curves, images, and all kinds of characters, including foreign letters and scientific symbols—by combining the dots in different ways. This eliminates the need for separate typewriter keys.

The advantage of a fully formed typewriter character is that it prints a crisp, sharp image. The dots laid down by the pins in a dot matrix printer can only approximate such crispness. One method in which dot matrix printers improve print quality is by double-striking when they print, the second time slightly off center so that the dots cover more paper area. Most dot matrix printers allow you to select either lower-quality one-strike printing (which is also faster) or higher-quality double-strike printing, depending on the job.

Monochrome (single-color) dot matrix printers are very popular, mainly because they're compact, reliable, and offer a wide selection of choices based on price and performance. There's no question: The least expensive PC printers available are monochrome dot matrix machines.

On the downside, dot matrix print quality may be adequate to good, but it falls short of the quality produced by laser printers. The shortcoming is especially pronounced when printing graphics. Also, many dot matrix printers can be deafeningly loud.

High-end 24-pin models (the more pins the higher the quality of the printing) can be had for between $500 and $1500; low-end 9-pin models go for as little as $150.

Color dot matrix printers are also available. They require special multicolor ribbons. Colors are limited, and the output is fairly primitive, though adequate for some purposes. Prices generally start around $500.

LASER PRINTERS Laser printers generate beautiful high-resolution output quietly and efficiently, delivering finished *cut paper* pages (discrete sheets) into a tray like a copy machine. Until very recently, laser printers were considered the Cadillacs—nay, the BMWs (Beamers)—of PC printers. A laser's what you aspired to after paying your dot matrix dues. But the cost of lasers has been falling so they're less expensive if no less desirable. The operating cost (cost per page) remains high, however, because like copy machines, lasers require expensive cartridges containing print toner, the laser equivalent of ink. Today, a number of models are available for around $1000. (The list price may be higher, but nobody pays list; see page 141.)

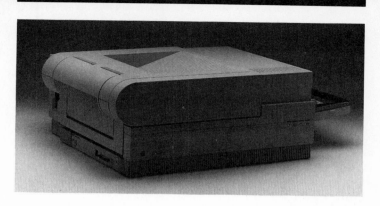

Laser printers are becoming more popular as the price drops. They are quiet and produce outstanding quality. In addition, they print single pages, eliminating the need for perforated track paper. (Photo courtesy of Apple Computer, Inc.)

EVERYTHING ELSE Once upon a time, *daisy wheel printers* —actually, typewriters without keyboards—were the king of the hill. They produce typewriter-quality print and they're inexpensive, if noisy. You can switch type-faces by switching daisy wheels. Unfortunately, daisy wheel printers suffer from one huge drawback: They can't print graphics.

Like laptop computers, *portable printers* are designed to pack and carry. They're compact, lightweight (generally under five pounds), and cute as a bug's ear. Most models are 9-pin dot matrix machines, though you may also encounter a few portable thermal and inkjet printers. If your work takes you far from an electrical outlet, be sure your portable has a battery option. Portables typically list for around $500.

Ink jet printers spray the paper with very fine, highly controlled jets of ink. These are much quieter than dot matrix printers. *Thermal printers* form characters and images by dragging a pin across specially treated paper. Before disgorging it, the printer heats the paper, exposing the scratched areas as text or graphics. *Thermal transfer,* or *thermal wax,* printers excel at producing crisp, full-palette color pages, but for a hefty price, from around $8000 upward to $16,000—prohibitive for most individual users and small businesses.

PERSONAL
COMPUTERS
FOR THE
COMPUTER
ILLITERATE

100

PLOTTERS

Plotters are used almost exclusively by architects, engineers, and technical artists to create elaborate, often very colorful floor plans, schemata, and illustrations. They're amazing tools; no hardware looks as spookily intelligent as a plotter at work.

Plotters are devices used to create multicolored architectural plans, maps, technical illustrations, charts and graphs, and other images on paper.
(Photo courtesy of Houston Instruments.)

There are basically two kinds of plotters: expensive upright models that plot on huge squares of paper, and lower-cost desktop alternatives. You plot in different colors by changing the pen or using a multipen model.

MODEMS

Like people, PCs may communicate via common phone lines. You can use your PC to send or receive text, graphics, numerical data, and even functional programs—applications. PC communications is certainly not an essential PC application, but depending on your livelihood and interests, it can be incredibly productive and even fun. I use my PC to send messages and to gossip with friends on the East Coast all the time. I also use it for work to send draft letters of agreement, to make travel arrangements, and to send queries and reports.

If you're interested in PC communications, you must have a hardware peripheral called a modem (rhymes with totem). Modem is a shortened form of the constipated compound term, *MOdulator-DEModulator*. It converts—modulates—computer information (text, graphics, or numerical data) to audio signals that can travel over conventional phone lines. Since the signals need some way of getting back into the computer on the receiving end, modems also reconvert—demodulate—them.

There are two kinds of modems: internal and external. *Internal modems* are simply enhancement cards that snap into one of the expansion slots inside the CPU. *External modems*, about the size of a paperback book, are about as exciting to look at as a TV channel changer; they're usually placed beside or on top of the CPU.

To use a modem, you have to connect it to your PC and to a phone line. Modems come in five transmission/receiving speeds, which are measured in *bits per second (BPS):* 300, 1200, 2400, 9600, and 19,200. Bits per second, sometimes called *baud rate* (baud rhymes with Maude), is roughly proportional to characters per second; a 2400 BPS modem can send the equivalent of a double-spaced page of text in seven seconds. The 1200 and 2400 BPS modems are the most common; 9600 and 19,200 BPS models are prohibitively expensive for most users. Modems can transmit and receive only as fast as the slowest of the two units involved in a PC communications session. So extra speed at your end is useless if the other end cannot match it. To use a modem, you need special communications software to convert the PC into a communications terminal (see "Communications/Electronic Mail/Fax," page 40).

NETWORKS

A network is a string of personal computers wired together, allowing users "on the net" to communicate with one another, share applications and hardware and devices (printers, modems, etc.), distribute data, or monitor each other's work on-line—among other things.

A newspaper, for example, might put all its researchers, reporters, writers, and editors on a network so that they can push copy back and forth as needed, ask questions of each other (without actually having to get on the phone or get up from their desks to track one another down), and comment on work in progress, as well as share access to in-house databases, printers, fax ma-

PERSONAL
COMPUTERS
FOR THE
COMPUTER
ILLITERATE

102

chines, and so forth. Networks range in size from a handful of PCs to hundreds of machines.

The curious thing about networks is they're not hardware, exactly; but then, they're not software, exactly, either. They're usually a synthesis of the two: enhancement boards, cables, network versions of common applications (database management systems, spreadsheets), and possibly even a specially configured PC set aside to regulate the entire system.

Networks have become increasingly important to business big and small. Companies value them because they enhance communications among staffers at all levels, and because, in allowing several or many PC users to share expensive hardware peripherals, especially high-resolution printers, they contribute to efficiency—and therefore the bottom line.

CD-ROM READERS

CD-ROM (Compact Disk/Read-Only Memory), the floppy and hard disks, is a medium for storing software. What sets CD-ROMs, also called optical disks, apart from floppies and hard disks is their phenomenal storage capacity. According to the magazine *PC Computing* (February 1990), Arthur Andersen & Company, the worldwide accounting and consulting firm, now uses a single CD-ROM disk, which looks exactly like an audio compact disk, to store what formerly amounted to a ton —literally, a ton, i.e., 2000 pounds—of printed manuals and documentation.

You cannot record (store software—applications and data) onto CD-ROMs, which is to say, CD-ROMs, like audio compact disks, are not erasable. This is why they're called "read-only memory." Erasable disks, often called *erasable optical disks*, are available, but the hardware required to run them remains prohibitively expensive for most PC users.

Still, CD-ROMs have a lot of appeal. A growing list of reference and educational materials is finding its way onto ROM disks. These include dictionaries (including the *Oxford English Dictionary*), thesauruses, almanacs, encyclopedias, directories, catalogs, and periodicals.

By compressing huge amounts of data, CD-ROMs save space and natural resources, and make stored data incredibly portable, as demonstrated by the Arthur Andersen example. In addition, you can sift through tons (literally) of stored information very quickly by conducting key-word searches or using some other electronic search scheme.

There's a hitch: To do these wonderful things, you need a hardware peripheral called a *CD-ROM drive* or *reader*, and they aren't exactly cheap (though they're a lot cheaper than the drives needed to operate erasable optical disks). The price will fall, however, as more materials are made available on CD-ROMs. Also on the horizon: commercially available multimedia CD-ROMs (and CD-ROM drives) that mix still and moving images and sound as well as text and numerical data. See also "Information Searches," page 44; "Multimedia," page 57.

ELECTRICAL APPLIANCES FOR THE PC

Personal computers not only need a continuous flow of electricity to work, they need a continuous flow of "clean" electricity. Throw a spike, surge, sag, or blackout into the line and who knows what could happen? Maybe nothing. Maybe an unexpected automatic shutdown and sudden loss of data. Maybe, horrible dictu, a PC version of a meltdown.

Actually, fried PCs are quite rare. In the first place, meltdown-grade electrical spikes and surges are simply not a routine phenomenon in North America. In the second place, most PCs have internal protection against all but the worst "overvoltages." In the third place, many users augment the PC's defenses by plugging all their computer equipment into a surge-protector power strip. These come in many configurations; I prefer those with on-off switches. This way I can turn all my equipment on and off with one tap of the foot.

The best defense against automatic shutdowns due to sags and blackouts (these are much more common than damaging spikes and surges) is saving current work to floppy disks or hard disks frequently (see page 154). Individuals and businesses that absolutely cannot afford to suffer downtime from power lapses can invest in *standby power systems* or *uninterruptible power systems (UPS)*, essentially sophisticated batteries equipped to augment standard power sources or compensate automatically for sudden loss of current.

PERSONAL
COMPUTERS
FOR THE
COMPUTER
ILLITERATE

104

FURNITURE/ACCESSORIES

Walk into almost any office supply store or that new phenomenon, office supply warehouse, and you'll find lots of PC paraphernalia, from the clever and useful to the inane. There are PC desks and tables and cabinets of all kinds, for example. These usually come with some combination of slots for receiving and dispensing printer paper, retractable platforms for keyboards and mice, boxy compartments for the monitor, and thoughtfully placed holes for stringing cables and power lines, among other considerations.

You'll also find floppy disk containers constructed of everything from practical if plebeian plastic to exclusive but enduring oak. There are plastic and canvas keyboard, monitor, and printer covers; monitor swivels, screen glare reducers; page holders (used to grasp paper documents and hold them in front of you while you tap on the keyboard or manipulate the mouse); designer mousepads (smooth placematlike surfaces for exercising your computer mouse); and all manner of stuff, some of it vital, some useful if not essential, and some just plain

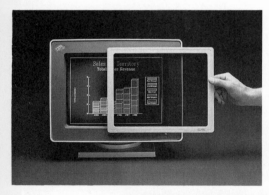

There are dozens of PC accessories available, including antiglare filters (left) and disk files (below). (Photos courtesy of Curtis Manufacturing Company, Inc.)

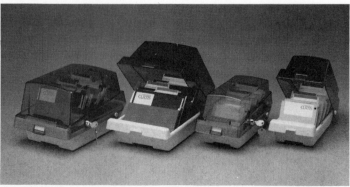

gimcrackery. To see what's available go into a store that carries this stuff—or examine it in catalogs or magazine ads. Chances are, you'll find some real problem solvers. Just wait, though, until you've actually started working at a PC and identified problems that need solving.

5

HOW TO CHOOSE A PERSONAL COMPUTER

There is no human problem which could not be solved if people would simply do as I advise. —GORE VIDAL

ABOUT THIS SECTION

Once you've decided you need or want a personal computer, prepare to weep. The PC marketplace is a seemingly impenetrable jungle of strange or alarming terms (disk cache, gas plasma display), unpronounceable or barely pronounceable acronyms (LCD, ASCII, GUI), and mysterious numbers (286, 386, 486). Blazing a trail through this dense undergrowth requires information, fortitude, and . . . a plan.

This section is divided in two parts. The first part, "All Things Considered," identifies key factors you should be aware of before making a buying decision. The second part, "The Choices," describes the types of personal computer—Apple II, IBM PC-compatible, Macintosh, IBM PS/2, and others—on the market today, and more important, discusses their relative advantages and disadvantages.

ALL THINGS CONSIDERED

THE STAGES

Selecting a personal computer that suits your needs and budget is best done by a process of elimination. The stages involved are familiar to anyone who's ever shopped for a new "sound system" in recent years.

CHOOSING THE COMPUTER TYPE First you select the type of computer system you want, but, following the sound system analogy, instead of choosing between a CD player, turntable, or cassette tape recorder, the choices are IBM-PC compatible, Macintosh, and IBM PS/2—or out of the mainstream, Apple II, Commodore Amiga, NeXT, and high-end machines called workstations.

A CD player, turntable, and tape recorder are all designed to play music, of course. But you can't play a CD on a turntable or a record on a tape recorder. CDs, in other words, are not compatible with turntables. Nor are records compatible with cassette recorders.

Just as turntables, cassette tape recorders, and CD players are all legitimate sound machines, the major different types of PCs are all bona fide computers, but there are differences in how they operate and in the applications they run. Like audio equipment, the different types of computers are not, with few exceptions, compatible with one another. You generally cannot run a Macintosh application, for example, on the IBM PS/2. For exceptions see "Compatibility," page 109.

CHOOSING THE BRAND Once you've selected the type of machine, the next step is to select the brand. This is actually simpler than shopping for a stereo, because you may have only one brand to choose from. For example, there's only one brand of Macintosh, the Apple brand—Apple, in other words, is the only company that manufactures Macintosh computers. Only IBM makes PS/2 computers. If you're shopping for an IBM-PC compatible (which I prefer to call DOS machines after their system software), however, there are dozens of manufacturers, big and small, who make the machine—not including, ironically, IBM itself, which stopped manufacturing IBM PCs in 1987 to concentrate entirely on PS/2s and, more recently, a so-called "home computer" called the PS/1.

PERSONAL
COMPUTERS
FOR THE
COMPUTER
ILLITERATE

108

CHOOSING THE MODEL After you've selected the type and brand of computer, the next step is zeroing in on a model. For some types, the model choices are blessedly limited (blessedly because life is simpler that way). For example, if you're in the market for a Macintosh, there are fewer than a dozen models to choose from. But for other types, DOS machines for example, there are hundreds of models to select among. Regardless of the type, the spectrum of choices usually ranges from less expensive, stripped down, and less powerful (slower processing speed) models to—you guessed it—very expensive, very powerful (fast) models packed with options.

CHOOSING THE OPTIONS Once you've decided on the type, brand, and model, what's left? In a word, options. This is America, after all, so naturally you have to negotiate a potentially treacherous mine field of options. A simple example follows. You've chosen a bottom-of-the-line IBM-PC compatible model, let's say, which comes with a monochrome (single-color) monitor and two floppy drives. You're offered the option of adding a color monitor and a 10-megabyte, 20 MB, 30 MB, 40 MB, etc., hard disk. You're also offered the opportunity to expand the machine's short-term memory, RAM.

Confusing? You bet. That's why it pays to become familiar in advance with the factors involved in choosing computer type, brand, model, and options. You can minimize confusion and frustration; arm yourself against aggressive, intimidating salespeople; save money; and zero in on the PC system best suited to your needs today, and next year.

CONSIDERING THE FACTORS

Many people know right away what type and model of personal computer they want: They want the same thing their neighbor or sister-in-law or golf partner uses. And you know what? This "affinity factor" is not necessarily irrational; it's just that other factors may be equally or more significant.

So take a little time to consider all the selection factors. Otherwise you risk contracting that most modern of maladies, digital regrets.

COST For most of us, cost ranks high as a factor influencing the type, brand, and model of personal computer we buy, not to mention the options we choose to add. If you have $10,000 to spend on a personal computer system, the world is your oyster; you can consider just about all the PC types. If you want to bring something home for under $1500, however, your choices will be much more limited, simplifying the selection process enormously.

Incidentally, when you budget for a system, remember that you'll almost certainly want a printer, which is usually sold separately. In addition, most software is sold separately and can be quite expensive. As with houses, automobiles, and many other big-ticket items, personal computers always end up costing more—sometimes quite a bit more—than the base price.

COMPATIBILITY If you work at an office that uses Macintoshes, and you're thinking of buying a personal computer for your home, chances are you'll want your home PC to be compatible with your office PC. This may seem obvious, but the compatibility factor isn't always so clear-cut. Consider the self-employed consultant who discovers she can get a fantastic deal on a Macintosh through a neighbor. Two months after bringing her new system home and learning the ropes, she discovers that most of her clients use PC compatibles, something she simply didn't become aware of until too late. Or what if you're buying a personal computer mainly for your kids. Does it need to be compatible with the computers they're learning to use at school? How about with their friends' machines (in case they want to lend each other games and instructional applications)?

The moral: Before committing to one type over another, look around and determine whether the compatibility factor should influence your choice.

ACCESS TO ASSISTANCE New York City, where I used to live, was deep in IBM territory (IBM PCs, PC compatibles, and PS/2s). Since I owned PC compatibles, I never had trouble finding help when I needed it. I could always locate someone—a friend, colleague, neighbor—who could supply the answer I was looking for.

When I moved to San Francisco, I became a stranger in paradise, having discovered that I'm one of the only independent users I know who works on an IBM-compatible. No kidding. Among independents, the

PERSONAL
COMPUTERS
FOR THE
COMPUTER
ILLITERATE

110

Mac appears to reign supreme in Baghdad-by-the-Bay. What's more, there are lots of neighborhood personal computer time-rental and desktop publishing services in this town, and they're stocked almost entirely with Apple Macs and Mac partisans. If they do happen to have an IBM PC or compatible, it's either a token or broken. I still have my IBM-compatibles and use them (I'm writing this book on one), but now I also have a Macintosh.

There's an important point to this parable: It's enormously helpful to have access to people who know more than you do about hardware and software. It's more helpful than books, classes, or blind faith. For some users, such access is critical. Given the limits of computer compatibility, however, an IBM PC-compatible expert is unlikely to know much about Apple IIs or Macintoshes. So, if you want access to real-life, hand-on-the-shoulder technical and operational help, stay close to the type of personal computer used by friends, colleagues, neighbors, and kind strangers. Or be certain there's a sympathetic dealer who will provide succor and guidance when needed.

EASE OF USE/USER INTERFACE I'm no "power user" (nor, like Prufrock, was meant to be). I'm not a wires-and-pliers type. I've got little aptitude or patience for hardware and software mysteries. As far as I'm concerned, the easier an application is to use, the better. My motto: Save time, avoid angst, live long, and prosper. Amen.

That hallowed but ill-defined quality, ease-of-use, in other words, is important to me—as it is to most personal computer users, newcomers and veterans alike. This quality, however, is not strictly an application-specific issue. It's also very much associated with type (PC-compatible, PS/2, Macintosh, etc.) of personal computer.

For example, almost from the day it was introduced, the Apple Macintosh has been considered the ease-of-use trail blazer. Every aspect of the Mac, from its scheme for plugging in peripherals (called "small computer system interface," or, more commonly, SCSI, pronounced "skuzzy") to the way Mac applications look and feel, was designed to make the machine easy to use—or as easy to use as possible, without sacrificing flexibility and performance.

At first, the Mac's ease of use was ridiculed by some, considered inappropriate for "serious" users. But today, most of the industry is engaged in a mad head-long rush to copy the Mac approach, especially its *graphical interface*—technically called the *graphical user interface (GUI)*.

The graphical interface has become a role model because it makes applications much more intuitive. Where old-style DOS applications often require you to type in commands, Mac apps represent commands on the screen with little pictures (called *icons*) or with simple, easily recognizable words. You activate an icon or word command by hitting designated keys on the keyboard or by pointing and clicking with a desk-top computer mouse. This simple approach relieves users of much of the tedious and time-consuming bur-den of memorizing commands or looking them up. It doesn't eliminate all confusion, but it certainly mini-mizes it.

The graphical interface is standard in all Macin-tosh applications. It is not standard in traditional DOS applications, however. If you want your DOS applica-tions to have a Mac-like graphical interface you have to equip your DOS machine with a special "applica-tion environment," of which there are several. The most widely used is called Windows. Only there's a catch or two. You can't equip low-end DOS machines with Windows, and you also need applications specifi-cally designed to run with Windows. If you use con-ventional DOS applications with Windows, they will look and feel just like conventional DOS applications —no graphical interface.

The upshot: Practically speaking, if you want to use applications with an easy-to-use graphical inter-face, you can buy an Apple Macintosh. Or you can buy a DOS machine, the Windows program, and Win-dows-specific applications.

PURPOSE/APPLICATIONS Just about everyone who knows anything about selecting a personal computer advises —admonishes is more like it—that hardware follows software. Translation: Don't commit to a personal computer type, model, or options until you've identi-fied your main purpose for buying a personal com-puter. In other words, consider applications first.

Why? Because personal computers are not created equally. Some makes and models are better suited for some purposes (applications) than other makes and models. Macintoshes, for example, are renowned for

PERSONAL
COMPUTERS
FOR THE
COMPUTER
ILLITERATE

112

the way they handle graphics applications and desktop publishing. (Macs are superb for lots of other applications, but they particularly shine when pictures are involved.) High-end DOS machines with warp-speed microprocessors are particularly appropriate for handling heavy duty "number crunching" applications— spreadsheets and statistics, for example. The Apple II line has long been considered a terrific (and inexpensive) machine for running educational programs or for introducing kids to personal computers.

PROCESSING SPEED Some personal computers compute faster than others. That is, they load applications (convert the PC to a specialized machine), call up files, and execute commands faster. This quality, processing speed, is often equated with power. When people talk about a powerful PC, they usually mean a fast PC.

Some PC users are speed freaks just for the thrill of it. Many others, especially those who use their computers for processing-intensive applications (spreadsheets, statistics, graphics), have a real need for speed-demon machines.

It undoubtedly goes without saying: Faster—more powerful—PCs cost more than slower PCs (sometimes a lot more). The good news: Most of us not only don't need a state-of-the-art bullet machine, we don't even need last year's state-of-the-art machine, at least not at any cost.

Processing speed is not something you're necessarily locked into when you buy a computer. Many personal computers are designed in such a way that you can enhance their processing speed later—at a cost, of course.

PORTABILITY Most personal computers are like other big-ticket home and office appliances: While they're not exactly immovable, once you plug them in, they're designed to stay put. Some makes, however, offer alternatives: portable PCs designed for the pack-and-carry set.

People who buy portable PCs typically use them to augment their desktop models. But there's no law against using a portable at home or in the office as well as on the road (or in the air, at the beach, or in your hotel room).

Some portables are just barely so. They're so heavy that their critics snickeringly, and appropriately, refer to them as "luggables." Others are incredibly compact, lightweight, and functional. As portables keep getting smaller, the industry keeps thinking up new terms to describe them: laptop computer, notebook computer, and now "palmtops." There's a limit, however, to downsizing. Who wants a matchbook-size PC screen (monitor) and a playing card-size keyboard?

Laptop computers come in many models. They are compact, lightweight, and, increasingly, every bit as functional as heavier, bulkier desktop PCs. (Photo courtesy of Toshiba.)

If you're looking for a machine you can use to do work on the plane or in similarly tight circumstances, not just any portable will do. A fourteen-pound unit may seem reasonable in the computer store, but what will it be like in real life when you're rushing pell-mell through the terminal to catch your flight clutching a garment bag and overcoat in one hand, a carry-on bag or purse (or both) in the other, and balancing a leaden, rigid so-called portable PC in the middle?

If you're interested in portable PCs, also be sure to check out battery life, screen quality, and keyboard design and dynamics in addition to size and weight before ambling out with your digital treasure.

Finally, the choice of portable models is just stupendous, as long as you go the IBM PC-compatible

**PERSONAL
COMPUTERS
FOR THE
COMPUTER
ILLITERATE**

114

route. Other types of computers either don't offer true portable models or offer very few.

RAM CAPACITY When you set out to buy a PC, regardless of the type, you'll notice that models are frequently distinguished from one another by "RAM capacity." RAM is random access memory, electronic work space that I prefer to call short-term memory. The varying amounts of RAM built into machines are measured in kilobytes or, if the capacity is large enough, in megabytes.

A quick refresher: To use system software and applications or existing data you have to transfer copies of them from long-term memory (floppy or hard disks, usually) to RAM. This is a simple, almost instantaneous, and sometimes even automatic procedure. Since the electronic work space is finite, however, you can put only so much software in it at one time. If an application is too "big," it won't fit in RAM. This is one of the reasons you need to know what applications you intend to run before you select a PC.

Fortunately, if you underestimate your RAM needs, you can have more RAM added to your system—or even add it yourself—at extra cost.

HARD DISK Not all personal computer models come with hard disks, a device for storing software (system software, applications, data) long-term, but these days, most do. And like RAM, hard disk capacity often helps distinguish one model from another.

There are two kinds of hard disks: internal (in the central processing unit) and external. The advantage of an internal disk is that it doesn't need extra desk space. Depending on the make of PC, it may use up one of the enhancement board slots, though. Like so many components, you can add a hard disk to the system later if you choose.

Hard disks come in different sizes, usually in increments of 10 megabytes. Hard disk size, or storage capacity, has become a macho thing. You can hardly be taken seriously these days as a PC user if you have less than 80 megabytes of storage. For my part, I don't know what people use all this capacity for. I've had a 10-megabyte hard disk since 1986, and I still haven't filled it up. But then, I don't store lots of applications on my hard disk (because I don't use lots of applications).

If you expect to use lots of applications regularly and to generate a huge amount of data, especially graphics, which take up more space, you'll want a larger hard disk. Average users, though, will get by quite nicely with 40 megabytes maximum.

FLOPPY DRIVES Depending on the make, some models of personal computer come with one floppy drive, others with two. Do you need two floppy drives? Strictly speaking, no, especially if you have a hard disk. But two is definitely handier than one, mainly because this gives you more flexibility in introducing applications and data to the system and in backing up data.

COLOR When Ted Turner started to "colorize" old black-and-white movies, Woody Allen and a handful of purists screamed bloody murder. Now I happen to be sympathetic to the position of Allen et al., but I also noticed that Turner's move was good business. People like color. This was borne out when a friend of mine who's a high school drama teacher told me that his classes howled and hooted when he announced his intention to show a black-and-white movie. "How," they demanded to know, "could anything in black and white be worth watching?"

Same with PCs. Most people, given the choice, prefer to see applications in color. If you're one of them, keep your eyes open when you start shopping for a system. Although color is rampant, it's not universal. And, of course, color generally costs more because you need a more expensive monitor and video enhancement board. Despite the extra cost, color monitors usually have lower resolution than monochromes. If you're on a budget, you can always start with monochrome and add color later.

BUNDLED SOFTWARE Many PC dealers, whether they sell from a store or via direct marketing (mail and telephone order from advertisements or catalogs), offer hardware-software combinations. In the business, this is known as "bundled software." The most common bundled software is system software, the master program every PC needs to operate. You're also likely to come across machines in which applications or utilities are offered "free with purchase."

Sometimes bundled software can make the difference between an okay deal and a good deal (or a good

**PERSONAL
COMPUTERS
FOR THE
COMPUTER
ILLITERATE**

116

deal and a great deal). But if the giveaway software is discontinued, disreputable (poorly reviewed), or if it's something you don't really need, then don't let it influence your buying decision.

ENHANCEMENT BOARDS AND OTHER FEATURES Enhancement boards are installed in central processing units to customize the system. One kind of enhancement board, an internal modem, for example, allows you to send and receive data over phone lines. Another optimizes video resolution on the monitor. Still another adds or enhances sound capability. A fourth acts as a hard disk drive. Depending on the type and model, some enhancement boards come as standard equipment, others as options. Be sure to ask about enhancement boards: Avoid paying extra for ones you don't need, understand, or want.

You're likely to encounter many other features, come-ons, and options when you start seriously shopping for a PC. If you don't understand what you're being offered, always insist on an explanation. If you don't understand the explanation, don't be intimidated; you can always take your business elsewhere.

THE CHOICES

There's no way I can describe all the personal computers currently on the market; there are far too many choices. New personal computers are introduced every week, and old ones discontinued. Even fat computer magazines published twice monthly can't keep up. So detailing the alternatives is not the object of these summaries.

Nor can I make a specific recommendation. Only you can define your interest and needs (" . . . start with applications").

Instead, the point of these summaries is to introduce you to key personal computer categories, to get you started, to point you in a direction. I emphasize the Big Three here—DOS machines (IBM PC-compatibles), the Apple Macintosh, and the IBM PS/1 and PS/2—because they dominate the market in unit sales and models, price, and feature options, and because most of the applications currently available or under development are designed to be used with these makes.

THE IBM PC AND IBM PC-COMPATIBLE FAMILY (DOS MACHINES)

There are hundreds of IBM PC-compatibles on the market. IBM itself stopped manufacturing IBM PCs in 1987, replacing its original product line with the PS (personal system) series. (Photo courtesy of Epson.)

PERSONAL
COMPUTERS
FOR THE
COMPUTER
ILLITERATE

118

The IBM PC-compatible category is the largest and most confusing of the Big Three. A little history explains why. Until the early 1980s, International Business Machines, Inc., was best known for manufacturing mainframe computers (the big ones) and electric typewriters. In late 1981, Big Blue, as the company has been known for years, surprised the world by introducing something completely different: a small, personal computer, the IBM PC.

In the next few years, Big Blue sold hundreds of thousands of IBM PCs, largely, if not exclusively, to corporate America. Other computer companies quickly sprouted, and using IBM PC technology, began selling their own usually cheaper versions of IBM PCs, the so-called *clones* and *compatibles.* (These days, "clones" and "compatible" describe the same thing, work-alike machines that can run applications and other software designed for the IBM PC.) This helped enlarge the market beyond big business because cheaper models attracted small companies, mom-and-pop enterprises, and independent users. By allowing these companies to use IBM technology, IBM also helped assure the dominance of its technical standards. Meanwhile, IBM held on to most of the big corporate customers, the so-called volume buyers.

Over the years, Big Blue introduced new models, including a portable unit (luggable was more like it), the PC-XT (for "extended technology"), and the PC-AT ("advanced technology"). In 1987, however, IBM discontinued the entire IBM PC line, replacing it with the PS (personal system) series (see page 124).

So today, IBM-brand PCs are no longer on the market (instead, IBM sells PS machines, which can run the same software as IBM PCs). No matter, for quite a few companies continue to manufacture IBM PC-compatibles (Compaq, Tandy, and Dell are three big names in compatibles). Most companies selling IBM PC-compatibles keep updating the original technology, offering machines that have advanced well beyond the IBM original. And many of these are regarded as superior to the true-blue real McCoy.

IBM PC-COMPATIBLES WRAPUP Most IBM PCS-compatibles offered are "286" or "386" machines. You'll also see a sprinkling of 486 and 8086 or 8088 systems. These numbers refer to the type of Intel microprocessor chip (the "heart of the brain") in the central processing unit (Intel is the name of the chip manufacturer). Early IBM PCs and compatibles (introduced in 1981–

82) used 8088 and 8086 chips. Succeeding generations employed the 80286 (introduced in 1984), 80386 (1986), and 80486 (1989).

But what do these numbers mean, exactly? In a word, speed—or in four words: pokey, fast, faster, fastest. Each succeeding microprocessor is faster than the one that came before it. In addition, each generation of PC is usually packaged with other bells and whistles like extra RAM (electronic work space), more hard disk capacity, and so forth.

Since it's axiomatic that the faster the processing speed of a PC, the better, it's easy to come to the conclusion that a 486 PC compatible is superior to a 386 machine (and a 386 machine to a 286 machine, etc.). The problem is, processing speed costs money, and few PC users, newcomers or veterans, can justify paying hundreds or thousands of dollars extra just to have a PC that contains the latest, fastest microprocessor. Besides, for the average PC user, buying the fastest PC on the market is like buying a Ferrari to drive your kids to school. It's overkill. So don't be awed by the fancy numbers; carefully consider your computer needs before choosing a model.

Also, keep in mind that microprocessing speed isn't the only thing that sets PC compatibles apart from one another. Manufacturers offer a near-infinite choice of models, each stuffed with a unique mix of features designed to meet the specific needs of individual users. Plus, you can usually customize systems in the same way you customize stereo equipment, by choosing and picking components and options.

GOOD NEWS/BAD NEWS

Good News: Since so many companies make DOS machines, there's *more product choice* in this category than among all the other personal computer types and models combined. Whether you emphasize processing speed, portability, color, or adaptability, you'll find lots of units to choose from.

Good News: *Genuine competition means good prices!* Of course, higher-end models cost more than lower-end machines, but whatever model you're interested in, there are some great deals to be made on PC compatibles.

**PERSONAL
COMPUTERS
FOR THE
COMPUTER
ILLITERATE**

120

Good News: There are *applications galore* (an estimated 50,000) for DOS machines, ten times more than for the make with the next richest lode of apps. (You should keep this impressive figure in perspective; few people use even a dozen applications, much less 5000 or 50,000.)

Good News: *DOS machines are everywhere;* at least, they're in more places than any other type of personal computer. So if you use a DOS machine, you will come as close to being omni-compatible, at least for the foreseeable future (perhaps for the rest of the decade), as it's possible to be.

Good News/   *A retrofitted graphical interface called*
Bad News: *"Windows" has been developed for DOS machines* by the same company, Microsoft, that sells DOS. Windows is basically a software scheme to make DOS machines look and feel more like Macintoshes—a terrific idea. But like most retrofits, Windows is only partly successful. Still, *you can buy a low-cost DOS machine installed with Windows, and get a Mac-like interface for less than the cost of a genuine Macintosh.* This is destined to become a popular choice for many PC newcomers. (You cannot, of course, run Mac apps on DOS machines, even if you have the Windows retrofit.) Also, you cannot run Windows on any DOS machine. It must contain a 286—or later generation—microprocessor. As a matter of fact, most experts today recommend a 386 machine for running Microsoft Windows.

Bad News: *DOS, the system software, and regular DOS applications*—in contrast to Windows applications—*are basically hostile to humanity.* They don't make much sense unless you're digitally inclined, which I certainly am not and most people I know are not. Of course, you can learn how to use DOS and DOS apps—I'm proof of that—but it's a struggle. And it shouldn't be.

Bad News: *IBM PC-compatibles are the most confus-*

ing business and consumer product on the planet! Figuring out how to load a new application on a hard disk, for example, or connect a new printer can be unreasonably difficult and time-consuming. Figuring out lots of things related to these machines is hard and time-consuming. This has a lot to do with their heritage (descended from IBM PCs, which are descended from mainframe computers).

THE APPLE MACINTOSH FAMILY

Apple Computer introduced the Macintosh in 1984, calling it the computer for "the rest of us." This was an only slightly veiled barb at IBM and its image as a remote, unimaginative corporate behemoth that built personal computers mainly for other unimaginative corporate behemoths. (Apple reinforced this interpretation when it broadcast a memorable Super Bowl commercial showing

Apple offers a number of Macintosh models. In general, Macintosh computers are considered the most accessible and easy-to-use of all personal computers available today. (Photo courtesy of Apple Computer, Inc.)

PERSONAL
COMPUTERS
FOR THE
COMPUTER
ILLITERATE

122

expressionless blue-suited office workers—that is, IBM PC users—stepping in single file lockstep off the edge of a cliff like so many lemminglike zombies.)

In fact, the Macintosh philosophy and design really did depart dramatically from the IBM PC (and compatible) standard. The original Mac built the CPU and monitor into a single box. The floppy drive accommodated 3½-inch disks rather than the prevailing 5¼-inch disks. Plus, on Macs, the mouse came as standard equipment. (Computer mice had been around for a number of years, but were largely viewed as novelty; the Macintosh changed that.)

A more radical departure from IBM's approach to personal computers became immediately apparent when you turned the machine on. With its graphical interface, simple word and picture commands, and point-and-click style of inputting, the Mac was definitely a departure from the IBM norm.

The first Mac was painfully slow, requiring many long seconds to call up an application or execute commands. It had only one floppy drive, no hard disk, and a small monochrome (single-color) monitor. Still, it caught on . . . like crazy, especially among individual users and younger people.

Initially, the Macintosh was lightly regarded by big business. This attitude changed as Apple introduced more powerful versions of the Mac and as more serious Mac applications became available (there are now more than 5000 Mac programs). Also, over time, corporate buyers learned to appreciate the Mac's built-in ease of use. The emergence of desktop publishing and the introduction of affordable—at least by business and professional users—laser printers gave the Mac a further boost, as its interface proved ideal for graphic design.

APPLE MACINTOSH WRAPUP The Mac is now available in a range of models. The most obvious distinction between the low end of the range and the high end is what they look like. The cheaper, less powerful versions are compact "classic" Macs. The CPU and monochrome monitor, in other words, are housed in the same box. In the pricier models, the CPU and monitor (monochrome or color) are discrete units connected by cables. High-end Macs also feature more RAM (electronic work space), greater capacity hard disks, and faster processing speeds.

GOOD NEWS/BAD NEWS

HOW TO
CHOOSE A
PERSONAL
COMPUTER

123

Good News: *There's absolutely no question: The Mac-*
intosh is the most inherently easy-to-use
personal computer on the market. This
quality is not limited to its famed graphical (point-and-click) interface. What
should be routine procedures like connect-
ing all the cables in a new system or installing applications on the hard disk or
setting up a printer *are* routine on the
Mac. Or at least, they're more routine—
straightforward, uncomplicated, and intuitive—than on other personal computers.
Plus, the Mac forces applications to use
consistent commands, eliminating the
need to learn lots of new commands every
time you use a new application.

Good News: *The Mac is fun.* Using it is pleasing. It literally chirps at you like a happy, well-fed
birdlet. It figuratively smiles, winks, and
scolds. It's responsive and friendly—in a
familiar human way, reflecting the high
value its designers placed on human engi-
neering. This might seem trivial, but I
don't think it's trivial at all. Because it
tries so hard to be unintimidating, the Mac
encourages users, even rank beginners, to
venture forth, explore, and learn more. At
its best, it's like an inspired teacher.
(Don't get me wrong, the Mac can also be
perplexing and aggravating, but its nature
is generally agreeable.)

Good News: The Mac was built to emphasize graphics.
Even low-end machines feature high-resolution displays. The result: sharp, detailed
applications and graphical data.

Good News: More than any other personal computer,
the Macintosh inspires enthusiasm and
loyalty among users. As a group, Mac
users seem more willing and even eager to
share knowledge and experience. Tapping
into such willingness can go a long way
toward helping complete computer illiterates advance rapidly.

Bad News: *Macintosh computers—and many Mac*

PERSONAL
COMPUTERS
FOR THE
COMPUTER
ILLITERATE

124

components—are generally more expensive than DOS machines. This is because Apple has a monopoly on Mac technology. In contrast, IBM PC technology is widely shared, fostering intense competition. Because only Apple manufactures the Mac, there is no competition; hence, the higher prices. Cost, however, is not the only measure of value. Many Macintosh owners justify the added expense by citing diminished technical difficulties and operational snafus—not to mention the value of a short learning curve and overall ease of use. Besides, when Apple cut the price of most Macintosh models in late 1990, it reduced, if not eliminated, the price advantage of many DOS machines.

Bad News: *There are ten times more DOS applications—about 50,000 at last count—than Macintosh apps.* From a practical viewpoint, this doesn't much matter to most users since 5000 provides plenty of choice. But the numbers also reflect the greater penetration, and according to some, vigor, of the DOS standard. There's no question that there are more DOS machines around, lots more, than Macintoshes.

Bad News: *Low-end Macintoshes tend to be sluggish,* requiring more time than most low-end DOS machines to initiate applications and execute commands.

THE IBM PERSONAL SYSTEM FAMILY (PS/1, PS/2)

When IBM introduced a new line of desktop computers in April 1987, it needed a name to distinguish the old PC products from the new. Hence "PS," short for personal system. Why did IBM abandon its famous, highly respected, and still thriving PC? The answer has as much to do with market share as with technology.

Big Blue wanted to make a break from the IBM PC market, a market it created, because there was too much competition. Initially, IBM was king of the hill, but over time, it saw more and more business, including corporate business, go to competitors who offered equivalent or superior machines at lower cost.

The IBM PS series of computers, which replaced the original IBM line in 1987, looks and operates much the same as its predecessor. In mid-1990, IBM introduced the PS/1 (shown), a model targeted expressly at home users. (Photo courtesy of IBM.)

Big Blue's solution was to develop a new personal computer, the PS/2, this time with more closely guarded technology. If other companies wanted to create PS/2 work-alikes, they could pay IBM a fee for the privilege. More recently, IBM introduced the PS/1, its so-called "home" computer. These machines are less powerful—and less expensive—versions of the PS/2 line. Fully DOS-compatible, they are suitable for many entertainment, instructional, personal interest, and business applications. Due to their built-in limitations, however, PS/1 computers may not be adequate for applications requiring large amounts of RAM or fast processing speed.

PS/2 WRAPUP If the Apple Macintosh is a paragon of simplicity—relatively speaking, anyway—the IBM PS/2 is just the opposite. Not that the machine itself is difficult to use; the fact is, the PS/2 looks and feels almost exactly like other DOS machines (PC-compatibles). This isn't surprising, considering that DOS is the standard system software for the PS/2. You can run any DOS application on a PS/2. You can also use install Windows, the retrofit Mac-like (graphical) interface created by Microsoft for DOS machines.

PERSONAL
COMPUTERS
FOR THE
COMPUTER
ILLITERATE

126

What complicates the PS/2 picture is the options and benefits claimed for the make. Even the experts are sharply divided about PS/2 pros and cons. The controversy centers on two aspects of the machine: microchannel architecture (MCA) and a new operating system called OS/2.

MCA was designed to increase processing speed, improve "linkage" between the central processing unit and peripherals, and allow for *multiprocessing,* running more than one application simultaneously, an important feature to sophisticated "power" users. Unfortunately, these benefits depend on development of new hardware products (expansion boards and peripherals). The new system software, OS/2, which comes with higher-end PS/2 models, is also supposed to play a part in delivering new benefits to users. The trouble is, critical advanced versions of OS/2 have been much delayed, as have OS/2-specific applications, though they are starting to become available. In any case, you are not limited to higher-end PS/2 models if you want to run OS/2. It will also perform as designed in properly equipped PC-compatible machines.

Besides, benefits similar to the ones promised by OS/2 are either already available or in the works for higher-end IBM compatibles and Macintoshes, further confusing the special status claimed for PS/2 machines. Still, the make is a fairly big seller, and most PS/2 users are happy with their choice. For the time being, most of them run them as DOS machines, very much like IBM compatibles. The range of IBM PS/2 models resembles the range of model choices for other types: Costlier high-end models come with faster processing speed, more RAM, more hard disk capacity, more slots for enhancement boards, and more standard features that are either sold separately for lower-end models or are not available at all. IBM has licensed other personal computer companies, including Tandy (Radio Shack), to manufacture machines incorporating PS/2 technology, namely its microchannel architecture.

GOOD NEWS/BAD NEWS

Good News: There's an old saying: No one ever got fired for buying IBM. Translation: IBM is no fly-by-night, here-today, gone-tomorrow outfit. *Big Blue,* in other words, *is safe and reliable.* The world—and IBM—have changed a good deal since this folk wisdom held undisputed sway. Still, many people feel more comfortable with those three little initials than with any of the alternatives.

Good News: *PS/2s have a smaller "footprint";* that is, they take up less desk space than most PC compatibles.

Good News/ Bad News: From the user's perspective, *PS/2s run very much like PC-compatibles,* that is, DOS machines. This is good because it means you can run DOS applications (and use DOS-created data). It's bad because if, from a practical viewpoint, there's no or little difference, then price becomes a bigger factor—and generally, PC-compatibles (in terms of processing speed, RAM, hard disk capacity, color monitor) cost less than equivalent IBM PS/2 models.

Bad News: *Most of the PS/2's claimed benefits,* related to microchannel architecture and OS/2, have yet to materialize. In any case, many of them are claimed for the high-end machines only (MCA and OS/2 are not available at the low end).

Bad News: Given all the claims, counterclaims, future benefits, real or imagined alternatives, newly minted acronyms, and the lack of agreement over the direction of PS/2 technology, *the IBM PS/2 is the most confusing make of personal computer;* considering the general chaos in the personal computer marketplace, this is quite a feat, from a consumer's point of view in any case.

THE APPLE II FAMILY

Today, Apple Computer, Inc., is best known for the Macintosh. But the company got its start eons ago (in 1976) when two young men, Steve Wozniak and Steve Jobs, took over a spare bedroom at Jobs's house to assemble computers from a design Wozniak had introduced earlier at the Homebrew Computer Club—in what soon came

PERSONAL
COMPUTERS
FOR THE
COMPUTER
ILLITERATE

128

to be known as Silicon Valley. A year later, the fledgling partners introduced the Apple II, a sophisticated—for its time—twelve-pound personal computer that helped create an industry, made the two Steves rich and famous, and is still in production.

Apple IIs may have been cutting-edge personal computers in the late 1970s, but today, many industry observers, if not users, consider them old hat. Most of the the action and innovation—and all of the glamour—at Apple is on the Mac side of the company. Still, Apple IIs are inexpensive, and many people who use them love them. They're terrific little starter machines, very popular in schools. There's a good deal of educational software available for Apple IIs, as well as games and basic home management and small business-oriented applications. On the downside, Apple II software is not compatible with anything else. Furthermore, many industry observers wonder how long Apple Computers, Inc., will continue manufacturing a make that accounts for so little of its overall business.

THE COMMODORE AMIGA FAMILY

The Commodore Amiga has attracted a nearly invisible but surprisingly large—and largely enthusiastic—following. The Amiga is generally inexpensive, all models come with color monitors (though these may be sold separately), and most standard applications (word processing, electronic spreadsheets, database, graphics, etc.) are available for the Amiga.

Unfortunately, the Amiga is widely viewed as a machine out of the mainstream of personal computing, largely because it lacks built-in compatibility with one or another of the two big PC currents, DOS (PC-compatibles and IBM PS machines) or the Mac. This is no problem for self-contained users who don't mind isolation. Anyone who wants or needs to swap applications and data files effortlessly with friends, the office, clients, neighbors, or other Amiga users (most of the rest of the world), however, should think twice before committing to the Amiga.

OTHER CHOICES

NeXT COMPUTER Steve Jobs, one of the founders of Apple Computer and the main man behind the Macintosh, left the company in a huff in the mid-eighties. Before long he announced a new company, NeXT, Inc. The NeXT Computer System, slick, jet black, and state-of-the-art-looking, does, in fact, go further than other consumer-oriented PCs toward incorporating cutting-edge technologies.

These include read/write/erasable optical disks. Like CD-ROMs, the NeXT's optical disks store vast amounts of software; but unlike CD-ROMs, which are "read only," they allow you to "write to the disk," that is, to store your own software on the disks (and erase it if you choose). Other features include CD-quality sound, and an innovative programming tool called NeXTstep that allows beginners to create or modify applications more easily.

The NeXT computer is very expensive, and for the time being, there's not a whole lot of software available for it. Because it's Steve Jobs's baby, many people expect great things from NeXT, Inc., but in time, in time.

WORKSTATIONS If you read the business press you've probably noticed lots of references to *workstations.* These are mainly very expensive souped-up personal computers targeted at engineers, publishers, scientists, software developers, and researchers. Most workstations use system software called Unix (yes, it's pronounced exactly like the word for castrated males in Europe and Asia). They have little relevance to most users and potential users.

FANCY CALCULATORS As the art of miniaturization advances, a number of companies have begun packing new capabilities—electronic calendars, memo pads, address files, and even simple built-in programs like spreadsheets and databases—into what used to be ordinary electronic calculators. Such handy little (and exquisitely portable) machines are typically billed as "personal computers." Which they are, technically. But beware: Unless they have a means of importing and exporting software that's 100 percent compatible with other machines (this is the role of floppy disks in standard personal computers), they're nifty, but extremely limited.

DEDICATED WORD PROCESSORS Many people buy PCs mainly to do word processing. There's an alternative. You may choose to buy a dedicated word processor, a type-

**PERSONAL
COMPUTERS
FOR THE
COMPUTER
ILLITERATE**

130

writer-like machine with a small built-in monitor and word processing software. The trouble is, you can't do anything else with it. A dedicated word processor is one specialized machine. A real personal computer is potentially dozens and dozens of specialized machines. So before spending hundreds of dollars on a dedicated word processing machine, be absolutely sure that you don't have other computing needs or interests—now or in the future.

6

PERSONAL COMPUTER HARDWARE AND SOFTWARE: HOW TO BUY SMART

Caveat emptor (Let the buyer beware).

ABOUT THIS SECTION

Under the heading "caveat emptor," in a terrific little dilettante's guide to Latin (*Amo, Amas, Amat and More*, Harper & Row, 1985), the author, Eugene Ehrlich, writes:

> Caveat emptor is the opposite of caveat venditor. Whereas caveat emptor has a long history in common law, caveat venditor is just now coming into prominence as a result of the consumer rights movement. Under caveat venditor, the seller is assumed to be more sophisticated than the purchaser and so must bear responsibility for protecting the unwary purchaser. The purchaser, emptor, is a child who must be protected against his own mistakes, while the seller, venditor, is the big, bad wolf lying in wait for Little Red Riding Hood.

I'm glad to learn the phrase, *caveat venditor*, and there's no doubt it has more relevance these days than in the past. But in the PC marketplace, caveat emptor is still the best advice.

Not that software and hardware sellers are a venal mob of rapacious cheats. As with most enterprises there are good and bad apples. The bigger problem is that the products are so complex and changeable, the technical ignorance of most PC users—not to mention sellers—so

PERSONAL
COMPUTERS
FOR THE
COMPUTER
ILLITERATE

132

pervasive, the stakes so high, and consumer protections so spotty or unenforceable that the motto must remain caveat emptor: Let the buyer beware. Make no assumptions. Arm yourself with information.

That's what this section is about, arming yourself in order to buy smart. "Sources of Information" points to common sources of information and help. "What's in Store for You" focuses on computer hardware and software retail stores. And "Buying Sight Unseen" offers advice about ordering products from catalogs, manufacturers, and other remote sources.

SOURCES OF INFORMATION

PERSONAL
COMPUTER
HARDWARE
AND
SOFTWARE:
HOW TO
BUY SMART

133

Believe me, more than for most purchases, it pays to spend some time exploring and understanding the options before buying PC hardware (including complete systems) and software. While hardware and software are not at all the same, when it comes to informing yourself about the choices, the same advice and precautions apply. Fortunately, it's not difficult to find useful, reliable information about hardware and software. What follows are summaries of standard sources of PC product information.

WORD OF MOUTH

"Friends, neighbors, colleagues, lend me your product expertise." That's certainly a reasonable—vital is more like it—motto for every PC user. Only the list of potential real-world enlightenment also includes taxi drivers, seatmates on airplanes, paper boys, cocktail party conversationalists, bridge partners, bowling buddies. . . . The fact is, anyone can turn out to be a valuable source of PC product information. You should exploit your fellow hominids to the hilt. Information from the user front can be the best kind of information, often much more germane and reliable than the overblown gushings or misguided counsel of people trying to sell you something.

If you're in the market for a word processor, for example, and you find yourself jawing with someone who uses MightyWord, quiz her relentlessly. How long has she been using PCs? What kind of work does she use MightyWord for? What, in her opinion, are its strengths and weaknesses? Is she familiar with other word proces-

PERSONAL
COMPUTERS
FOR THE
COMPUTER
ILLITERATE

134

sors? If yes, how does MightyWord compare? If she had it to do over again, would she still opt for MightyWord?

When quizzing people about hardware and software, always determine their biases. And use common sense. If your source is a tough-skinned PC veteran who raves about MightyWord because "it isn't contaminated by wimpy ease-of-use considerations," you might do well to steer clear of MightyWord, or at least get a second opinion (or better yet, a demonstration; see "Product Demos," page 140) before rushing out to buy.

USER GROUPS

Computer clubs, called user groups, are democracy in action, people with a shared need or interest coming together regularly to exchange information and provide mutual support. User groups have proliferated in the past decade so that today they're common even in smaller towns and rural areas. There are also special user groups affiliated with schools, companies, government agencies, or focusing on particular PC systems (the Macintosh, for example) or on applications (animation, electronic spreadsheets, desktop publishing, etc.).

Many user groups offer members free or inexpensive classes, hardware and software swaps, product demonstrations, publications, discounts on hardware and software, access to technical and operational gurus, and a lively program of guest speakers. Larger personal computer user groups are subdivided into *special-interest groups (SIGs)*, which meet separately, often before general meetings, to share information on specialized topics ranging from occupations (accounting and tax preparation, consulting, education, law, religious organizations) to general applications (computer-aided design, communications), specific applications (Lotus 1-2-3, Word-Perfect), technology (CD-ROM, voice), avocations (genealogy/family history), and social concerns (the disabled and computers, nonprofit computing).* User groups large enough to organize special-interest groups usually include one especially for PC newcomers.

* These examples are a partial list of SIGs from the New York Personal Computer user group, NYPC.

PERSONAL COMPUTER MAGAZINES/NEWSPAPERS/BOOKS

PERSONAL
COMPUTER
HARDWARE
AND
SOFTWARE:
HOW TO
BUY SMART

135

Many people complain that personal computer magazines are "nothing but ads." This is an understandable impression, but it's not true. Most computer magazines are at least 40 percent editorial. In a 300-page magazine —they're often this big or bigger—40 percent equals 120 editorial pages; that's almost book length.

The problem with computer magazines is that, at first glance, they seem so daunting, filled with strange words, unfathomable technical advice, recondite technical illustrations, and opinion columns addressing obscure controversies you've never heard of.

But most product-oriented computer magazines devote many pages—even entire issues—to hardware and software reviews. The best of these mix objective analysis based on product testing with subjective human appraisals based on hands-on experience with the product. All this independent information is presented in one convenient place, frequently accompanied by surprisingly lucid explanations (often including a glossary of terms) and comprehensive product feature tables.

So while an entire computer magazine may appear formidable and off-putting, a particular review article within an issue can be tremendously helpful. The thing to do is look these magazines over at the newsstand or in the library, turning right to the table of contents. If the issue contains a review of a product category you're interested in—word processors, modems, 386 DOS machines, monitors, printers, business graphics software— check it out, ignoring all the other advanced stuff in the magazine. You may be surprised to find the review that caught your eye is more than worth the price of the issue. Besides, the ads themselves can also be unexpectedly informative, especially if they address hardware or software products that interest you.

Many daily newspapers publish PC-related opinion columns, product reviews, guides to user groups, classes, and swaps. In some cities local publishers distribute fat fortnightly or monthly tabloids devoted entirely to PC products and consumer issues—free. If you come across one of these—they're distributed in shops and curbside dispensers—pick one up. You've got nothing to lose.

Most personal computer books—unlike this one— address a specific system software (DOS, Windows, OS/2), computer (Macintosh, Apple II, PC-compatible), application (Lotus 1-2-3, Pagemaker, WordPerfect), lan

PERSONAL
COMPUTERS
FOR THE
COMPUTER
ILLITERATE

136

guage (BASIC, Assembly, C), or occupation (accounting, teaching, medicine). Most of them are scandalously overpriced. And many are incomplete, badly written, poorly organized, or all three.

There *are*, however, terrifically useful books available. Arthur Naiman's *The Macintosh Bible* (Goldstein and Blair, 1988–89), for example, rates very high in my estimation, especially for green, largely uninitiated Macintosh Computer users. David O. Arnold's *Getting Started with PCs and Compatibles* (Brady, 1988) offers an accessible, illuminating, genuinely helpful introduction to users of DOS machines.

Most bookstores these days have a computer section. Go and browse. If you have a particular need, please don't buy on the fly or you'll probably regret your choice (this is experience talking). There must be at least three dozen DOS books on the market at any one time, for example, but they vary wildly in quality and practical usefulness.

HARDWARE AND SOFTWARE COMPANIES

Most companies that sell hardware and software are only too happy to provide printed product information, usually a good deal more than you want. All you need is an address or phone number, which is easy to find if the companies advertise. Don't expect this information to be 100 percent objective, though; after all, it's intended to make a sale. Still, it can be useful, detailing product features and capabilities. Application publishers sometimes offer *demonstration disks* (software product samples), free or for a nominal fee. These can give you a sense of the look and feel of the program, as well as a limited preview of its capabilities.

HARDWARE AND SOFTWARE STORES

Retail outlets that sell applications and other software, computer systems, and peripheral hardware are obvious sources of product information. Unfortunately, the quality of information is wildly, absurdly—criminally—uneven. On the one hand, it's just amazing how uninformed or worse, ill informed, so many staffers are at hardware and software stores. So be careful; switch on your critical faculties when soliciting information from retail outlets. If in doubt about accuracy, get a second opinion.

On the other hand, many staffers are well informed, willing to help, and capable of explaining complex features and capabilities in simple English. If you happen upon such earthly saints, offer them praise, gifts, gratitude, and marriage. In short, seek answers from them, but treat them well.

OTHER SOURCES

Once you start paying attention, you're likely to notice ads and announcements publicizing the services of inexpensive computer classes (general and application-specific) offered privately and through local colleges. Computer fairs, expositions, and swap meets open to the public are common in many cities. And increasingly, young personal computer experts are going into business for themselves, offering their expertise for a sometimes hefty hourly fee. An hour's worth of individualized attention can be a real bargain, though, if it saves a day, a week, or your sanity.

PERSONAL
COMPUTER
HARDWARE
AND
SOFTWARE:
HOW TO
BUY SMART

137

PERSONAL
COMPUTERS
FOR THE
COMPUTER
ILLITERATE

138

WHAT'S IN STORE FOR YOU

Once you decide you want a personal computer or any other products in the vast, expanding universe of PC hardware, software, and accessories, you've got to decide where to buy it. The choices are legion. There's also a thing or two, though—a caveat or two—you should know about how to buy PCs and PC-related products.

Hardware and software retail outlets range from antiseptic showrooms designed to appeal to the jaundiced eye of big-budget corporate buyers to traditional mom-and-pop office supply stores that saw the handwriting on the wall and added computers, peripherals, software, and accessories to their line of goods. I've even seen Macintoshes for sale in a cosmetics store.

Generalizing about the pros and cons of different retail options is risky. While the staff at one nationwide retail store may be completely indifferent to individual customers, the staff at a sister franchise across town may go out of its way to answer questions and demonstrate equipment. A mom-and-pop shop that looks like something out of a prewar Jimmy Stewart movie may provide the best follow-up technical and operational assistance within a hundred miles.

So what follows are guidelines for buying PCs and PC products retail in person. Most of the advice applies regardless of where you decide to do your "trading," as my rural Texas grandmother used to call it.

ADVICE FOR ALL SITUATIONS

These tips apply to all products, hardware, software, and accessories, whether you're browsing, researching the options, or know exactly what you want.

COMFORT AND UNDERSTANDING If you find yourself the unwilling target of a fast-talking, jargon-spouting, hard-selling salesperson, don't hesitate to leave. But do us all a favor and let the jerk know why you're leaving.

Unfortunately, this breed continues to flourish, evidently because the hard sell sometimes works. But whether you're a regular or a potential customer, whether you're buying thirty new top-of-the-line machines for a corporate office or a low-priced starter machine for yourself, you have a right to expect patience, consideration, and clear answers. Of course, you have a responsibility, too. Don't pretend to be what you're not; if you're a newcomer, say so. Make it plain that you need explanations and objective guidance.

Don't expect salespeople to know *all* the answers. But they should be knowledgeable about all the products they sell—or find someone in the store who is. If the staff at a store is ignorant about its stock, or worse, is ignorant, but pretends not to be, walk on by.

PERSONAL
COMPUTER
HARDWARE
AND
SOFTWARE:
HOW TO
BUY SMART

139

SHOP WHERE SATISFIED FRIENDS, NEIGHBORS, AND COLLEAGUES SHOP
The Honda Civic sells well year after year mainly because people who buy Honda Civics consistently tell everyone they know how well made their cars are, how trouble-free they are, how much fun they are to drive, what great service they get from the dealer, and so on. Word of mouth, in other words, is powerful—and usually, if it comes from more than one source—reliable. So keep your ears tuned, or better yet, be proactive and ask around. If you hear that the Summit Computer Store is tops, head on over and have a look around for yourself. And be sure and tell them why you're there.

COMPARE PRICES... Comparison shopping definitely pays
when it comes to personal computers and peripheral hardware. If you know exactly what you want, call around to various dealers and get their best quotes. Then play the two best deals against each other (this is just like shopping for a car). There's no guarantee, but depending on the product, haggling can knock as much as 20 percent off the asking price, at least for whole systems and other big-ticket purchases.

...BUT REMEMBER, PRICE IS NOT THE ONLY MEASURE OF VALUE Thou-
sands of people make a pilgrimage to an impressively frenetic, incredibly seedy-looking computer and electronics store in New York City that's justifiably famous all over the country for its wide selection and low prices. But good luck getting an unrushed product demonstration there or finding someone to explain the essentials of hard disk management two weeks after cutting your deal. I'm not knocking this joint, not at all (I'm a satisfied customer). My point is that other qualities, such as individualized attention and access to postpurchase assistance, may be just as important to you as rock-bottom prices.

PERSONAL
COMPUTERS
FOR THE
COMPUTER
ILLITERATE

140

BE WARY OF PRICE CLAIMS AND WATCH FOR HIDDEN COSTS The computer hardware and software business is no different from most other businesses. Some dealers make outrageous, insupportable claims, called "lies" in plain English. So don't accept advertised price claims at face value; read the small print and ask questions. If you do, you may discover enough conditions and exclusions to render the we-won't-be-undersold rhetoric completely meaningless. For example, one dealer may sell a particular brand of PC at the lowest price around, but impose a mandatory "assembly fee" or charge separately for the monitor and keyboard or be forever out of stock with that model. Another may promise to beat the competition . . . except for mail-order purchases or items purchased later than last week.

PRODUCT DEMOS Many hardware and software stores offer upon request their own version of test drives—namely, product demonstrations. Of course, if you're already familiar with a particular product, a demo is superfluous. But it's reasonable to expect an opportunity to try out a new PC or a printer or an unfamiliar application before making a decision. If a store doesn't offer demos of every product it sells, go to one that does.

Many software stores will "break the shrink wrap" of an application or other software product if that's what it takes to satisfy your curiosity. This service, of course, is of limited value if the store doesn't have whatever on-site PCs and peripheral hardware are necessary to demo the capabilities and features of all the software it sells.

CONFIRM THE WARRANTY PC hardware and software typically come with manufacturer's warranties guaranteeing replacement (software) or parts and labor (hardware). For a number of products, however, especially big-ticket hardware items, warranties are valid only if you buy the products from an authorized dealer. Since many discount dealers and catalog supply houses are not authorized dealers, you might risk losing the manufacturer's warranty when you snare a good deal. In some cases, dealers compensate by tossing in their own warranty. If this is the case, make sure it's equivalent (parts *and* labor for hardware) before you buy. You can get lists of authorized dealers, incidentally, by calling manufacturers directly.

When you buy hardware and software, take care not to void the warranty unintentionally. Some manufacturers consider their warranties voided, for example, if you remove the case housing the central processing unit or if you have repair work or upgrades done by other than an authorized technician.

PERSONAL
COMPUTER
HARDWARE
AND
SOFTWARE:
HOW TO
BUY SMART

141

VOLUME PURCHASES If you're planning to buy more than one of anything—personal computers, peripherals, or applications—definitely ask about price breaks. Better yet, ask around about price breaks, engaging in the same kind of comparison shopping you would if you were looking for one measly dot matrix printer.

LIST PRICE Most people know that "no one pays sticker price" when buying a new car. The same is generally true for PC hardware and software: No one pays list price. More accurately, for many products, especially applications software, one need not pay list price. A big exception: mail-order private-label hardware.

Some hardware and software companies and retailers offer schools, nonprofit organizations, artists, teachers, college students, the elderly, the disabled, and other worthy users special discounts and terms, even on individual purchases.

A NOTE ABOUT OBSOLESCENCE The criminally misleading word "obsolescence" gets tossed around a lot in the PC business. It's typically used to frighten people into buying more hardware and software or more expensive hardware and software than they need. Whenever you hear or read this word or a variation, turn your critical thinking capacity up to Maximum Alert.

Yes, it's true, as hardware and software evolves, you may find the products you bought or are thinking of buying are not as fast or fully featured as the newest products on the market. In addition, it's likely that, with the passing of enough time, your PC won't be able to accommodate the newest, fastest, most fully featured hardware and software unless you upgrade your system. This, according to many marketing wizards, makes your equipment obsolete.

As far as I'm concerned, however, nothing is obsolete as long as it does what I want it to do. My PC is

PERSONAL
COMPUTERS
FOR THE
COMPUTER
ILLITERATE

142

not state-of-the-art. My word processor is ancient. My floppy drives are old-style 5¼-inchers. I could go on and on. Funny thing, though, my PC still works fine. If, at some point, I want a program that needs more RAM or more hard disk storage, I'll look into an upgrade. Until then, there's absolutely nothing obsolete about this old gray mare; she's everything she used to be.

BUYING APPLICATIONS

These buying tips apply to software only.

IT'S WHAT'S INSIDE THAT COUNTS Don't be seduced by slick packaging, heavy advertising budgets, or splashy in-store displays. I've come across applications packed in boxes so plain, so lacking in any kind of design sensibility, so plug-ugly, that they look, on the face of it, beneath consideration. Yet some of these apps have earned nothing but raves from product reviewers and users alike, including me.

CHECK SYSTEM REQUIREMENTS... You have a DOS compatible. You're looking for a particular DOS-compatible application. You find it. You buy it. Simple, *non?* Well, maybe not so simple. Virtually every application sold comes with a list of minimum *system requirements* dealing with RAM capacity, color, availability of a hard disk, type or version of system software, and so forth. If your machine does not meet just one of those requirements, the application may not work, or if it does, it may not work as well as expected. So you should know your system and always check the system requirements (printed on the package) before buying.

...AND BE SURE YOU'RE GETTING THE LATEST VERSION System software, applications, utilities, languages, most software products, in other words, are revised from time to time in order to add features and eliminate bugs. Be sure, when you buy, that you're getting the most current version of the software available. Some stores discount discontinued versions of applications, so pay particular attention when the price is unusually low.

AVOID BUGGY SOFTWARE Be on the lookout for poorly designed or buggy applications. Warning signs are an inconsistent look and feel, inconsistent use of input devices (some commands work with a mouse, others don't, for example), and slow response for some commands and processes in otherwise speedy programs. If you know what to look for, these tip-offs can all be spotted during a product demo. Also check the manual. Lots of correction pages or complex instructions for what should be fairly routine operations should give you pause. Try to track down relevant product reviews or tap into your word-of-mouth network if you're unsure of a software product's quality.

PERSONAL
COMPUTER
HARDWARE
AND
SOFTWARE:
HOW TO
BUY SMART

143

SITE LICENSING It is illegal to buy one application and make 20 copies of it for the office. Many application publishers, however, offer *site licensing agreements*, arrangements authorizing users to make a limited number of copies for a fee.

BUYING HARDWARE

These buying tips apply to hardware, including PC systems, only.

RENTING In most cities you can rent desktop and laptop personal computers, printers, hard disks, modems, plotters, network systems, scanners, multimedia systems, and other specialized peripherals by the hour, day, week, month, or for longer periods. Most rental suppliers will also provide software if needed.

Renting can be an excellent way to try out equipment, expand computer work capacity rapidly, or computerize a distant vacation house. If you rent, ask about pickup and delivery, installation, software loaners, and on-site technical support. To find computer rental companies, look under "Computer" in the Yellow Pages.

USED PERSONAL COMPUTERS Increasingly, when people move up to more sophisticated computers they trade in the old ones, sell them to friends or acquaintances, or give them away. So if you prefer to buy a used PC, you can probably find one. To find what's available, do the usual thing: Ask around, checking the classified and bulletin boards, and with friends, local user groups, and PC dealers.

Used machines are an attractive alternative to many people. The potential problem with hand-me-

PERSONAL
COMPUTERS
FOR THE
COMPUTER
ILLITERATE

144

down PCs, of course, is that they ordinarily don't come with any kind of guarantee or warranty. And like most contraptions, personal computers don't last forever; they wear out, or at least, critical components like floppy drives, hard disks, fans, input devices, and monitors wear out.

Many hardware components receive an *MTBF— mean time between failure*—rating from their manufacturers. In plain English, MTBF means "average life span." If key components of the used PC you're thinking of buying are approaching or have exceeded their average life span, you could be in for major downtime sooner than you think. Unfortunately, some components, once they've gone down—"gone dead"—cost more to revive than brand-new equivalent equipment.

BUILDING YOUR OWN The idea of building your own PC is perennially appealing to a tiny group of wires-and-pliers-oriented users. This actually is not terribly difficult as there are only about twelve components involved, all commonly available. At best, though, you stand to save about one-third off the cost of a new equivalent machine. Assembly could easily take half a day, not counting time spent researching and searching for components. For my part, dueling with those do-it-yourself demons, Confusion, Error, and Paralysis, is not worth the dubious satisfaction of starting from scratch.

BUYING PCs, HARDWARE, SOFTWARE, AND ACCESSORIES SIGHT UNSEEN OR HOW TO BE A HAPPY DIRECT MARKET CUSTOMER

PERSONAL
COMPUTER
HARDWARE
AND
SOFTWARE:
HOW TO
BUY SMART

145

You can get anything you want . . . by picking up the phone, dialing an 800 number, and reciting your credit card number. You can get, for example, a brand new state-of-the-art PC system. Or maybe you're interested in a particular system component like a monitor or an enhancement board or a hard disk. How about a new printer? Or an application? Or a box of blank floppy disks?

Direct marketing of PC products is big business. Many people, on the one hand, are quite reasonably wary of buying hardware and software this way, especially the big-ticket items. They're right to be wary. On the other hand, if you take precautions and know exactly what you want, ordering sight unseen can offer compelling advantages.

Chief among these is price. Direct marketers make their money on volume rather than markup. Another key advantage is convenience; you can order from home or office. In addition, direct marketers tend to offer wide (even vast) selections and fast delivery, often including overnight delivery for smaller items (for an extra fee).

Ordering from direct marketers is far from fail-safe, though. You can increase your chances of avoiding consumer grief by taking simple precautions, described below.

SIZE UP THE COMPANY FIRST Don't order from companies you know absolutely nothing about. For guidance about which direct marketing suppliers are reputable, talk to other users. (Users groups are especially rich lodes of where-to-buy/where-to-avoid information.) You can also check with government consumer agencies, the Chamber of Commerce, or the Better Business Bureau in the company's city. Keep a record (date, time, name of representative at the other end of the line, details of the conversation) in case you do have problems later on.

INSIST ON A RETURN POLICY AND OTHER GUARANTEES Avoid all-sales-are-final companies like the plague. The fact is, reputable direct marketing companies understand the wariness of potential customers and bend over back-

PERSONAL
COMPUTERS
FOR THE
COMPUTER
ILLITERATE

146

ward to earn trust. Their efforts include, for PCs and other hardware products, thirty-day (typically) no-questions-asked guarantees (at seller's discretion thereafter), toll-free technical support, warranties on parts and labor (including return freight costs), and free or optional on-site service for PCs and hardware.

Software guarantees are usually more limited since unscrupulous customers could abuse liberal return policies by copying applications and then returning them for a refund. Reputable direct marketers of software products, however, always guarantee against defects, (not the same as bugs, glitches associated with design and programming rather than manufacturing and shipping).

SIGNS OF TROUBLE Avoid ordering from companies that don't offer an 800 toll-free phone number, that don't advertise regularly in the same place (usually magazines), or whose advertisements lack a street address (a post office box number doesn't qualify). When you call in your order, if the person at the other end is rude, sounds tentative, or can't answer your questions (or refer you to someone who can), say "So long."

ASK QUESTIONS AND BE PRECISE Know exactly what you're ordering, and confirm that all the features and components you expect are included in the price. If you're interested in a PC, for example, be sure it comes with a monitor (sometimes "PC" refers to the central processing unit only). Ask about additional fees, taxes, shipping charges, or surcharges for credit card purchases. Avoid companies that charge a "restocking fee" for taking back returned merchandise. This penalizes you for being dissatisfied.

BE SKEPTICAL OF "STEALS" If prices are unbelievably low, then don't believe them. How can you tell? If they're substantially lower than prices for identical products offered by other direct marketing suppliers, you should be suspect.

USE PLASTIC Always pay by credit card. This may give you the option of withholding payment if the merchandise fails to show up or proves grossly unsatisfactory. It also may provide extra protection against defect or loss (some credit cards, for example, double the length of the merchandiser's guarantee).

7

AN OUNCE OF PREVENTION AND SIMPLE CURES: TIPS FOR NEW USERS

Nobody knows the trouble I've seen. Nobody knows but me.
—TRADITIONAL SPIRITUAL

ABOUT THIS SECTION

My friend Kate has a PC, an IBM-compatible that she bought mainly for word processing. Kate had a dreadful experience with her PC that was similar to the experience of many users, especially newcomers.

Here's what happened. One morning Kate turned on her machine, could hear it purring, but nothing appeared on the screen. Something was obviously wrong, terribly wrong. She was on deadline. This was the last thing she needed.

Kate's husband, Rick, got involved. They hauled the whole shebang, CPU and monitor, to a shop they had located after making half a dozen phone calls. They left the machine there. The next day, the $35-an-hour technician called to say that they would get better results if they turned on the monitor. It seems Kate had inadvertently turned it off the day before. She didn't realize that the monitor had a separate on-off switch. All she knew was that in the past the damn thing came on every time she turned on the central processing unit.

Kate and Rick brought the computer home and set it

PERSONAL
COMPUTERS
FOR THE
COMPUTER
ILLITERATE

148

up. When they turned it on, the monitor displayed nothing but evil diagonal static. Woe unto Kate, she was sure all that jostling had broken something deep inside her PC. Rick—young, urbane, smart, successful, self-confident, good-looking, well educated, the product of a happy childhood, and a complete idiot when it comes to personal computers—got back on the horn to the repair saint. Frantic, he described the problem. The technician said, "Well gee, I dunno. Have you tried the vertical hold?" Rick looked for, found, and adjusted the vertical hold knob. Wonderful to say, the evil static was exorcised. Kate's PC, never sick, was well again.

This is a true story. And a common one. Obviously, it has a moral, namely: When your PC does something unexpected (like refuse to work properly), don't automatically assume the worst. There may be a simple explanation. This short section is about simple explanations and simple precautions you can take to avoid trouble with your PC in the first place. Precautions first.

AN OUNCE OF PREVENTION

AN OUNCE
OF
PREVENTION
AND SIMPLE
CURES: TIPS
FOR NEW
USERS

149

Listen, friends, I know most of us learn lessons the hard way, painfully, full of regrets, fiercely determined to do better, to shed our natures, to have victories over ourselves, to avoid avoidable mistakes next time, alas. Oh, yes, very occasionally, a bit of good advice, a well-placed warning, some wise counsel actually penetrates the enameled carapace of our smiling self-delusion, deflecting us from some inconvenience or disaster. But rarely, friends. Rarely.

The following tips are like religion to those of us who've suffered the consequences of not taking them to heart early in our PC careers. Because there's still hope for you, I offer them here.

- *Get a personal guru—or gurus.* You know, someone who knows more about your system and your key applications than you. Many times this is a smart, motivated kid with a flair for PCs. It can also be a friend or neighbor or a new acquaintance at the local user group. It's often a local dealer who's not only willing to be helpful, but enjoys doing so. Nothing helps users more than having a fellow human to call on for PC-related assistance and advice.

PERSONAL
COMPUTERS
FOR THE
COMPUTER
ILLITERATE

150

• *Handle your equipment gently from the start.* It looks sturdy and it's true, there aren't very many moving parts. But just because the innards are largely immobile doesn't mean they're not delicate. They are. So take care.

• *Send in all warranty/registration cards.* This won't prevent your system from phasing out, but it may assure a healthy response from the manufacturer if it does go down.

• *Save your boxes, packing material, and other odd-looking bits of cardboard and foam that come with your PC and any hardware you buy.* In the short run, you may want to return your system. In the long run, you almost certainly will want to move or store or sell or ship your PC someday. When that day comes, you'll be very glad you have the original boxes and packing materials. Trust me on this one.

• *If you move your PC, be sure to protect the hard disk and floppy disks.* When you bring your PC home, you're likely to find removable squares of cardboard inside the floppy drives. Save these and reinsert them if you ever move the system any distance or put it in storage. You may also need to "park the head" of your hard disk before moving it. Check your manual or ask your personal digital guru about the procedure for doing this.

• *Don't block vents on your central processing unit or monitor or anything else that has vents.* The vents are there for a reason, to help keep the inside cool. If you block them, the equipment can't breathe, and like you and me, it needs to breathe to live.

• *Keep all liquids away from your computer.* Do not set glasses or cups of anything on or near the monitor, the CPU, the keyboard, the printer, or other peripheral devices. Liquids are conductors of electricity. Spilling water or wine or coffee on an active keyboard is like fusing all the circuits under the keys and sending your PC a dozen commands at the same time. Taking your keyboard apart to dry it out or parting with the bucks to buy a replacement may not be such a big deal, relatively, but a cup of tea spilled into the vents of your CPU . . .

• *Handle floppy disks with care.* Don't jam them into floppy drives; insert them gently. Never try to insert a floppy into—or remove it from—an active disk drive (indicated by a light, by a gentle grinding sound, or both). Always keep floppies in their protective sleeves when not in use. When I first started using 3½-inch disks, which come in rigid plastic cases, in contrast to the soft plastic of 5¼-inch diskettes, I thought, "Oh, these are great, virtually indestructible." I would toss them into my jacket pocket naked, without the sleeve. Hard-earned lesson: Sand and fluff found its way from the inside of my pocket to the floppy and from there to the disk drive itself, necessitating expert cleaning that, fortunately, saved the data. So I repeat, always keep floppies in their protective sleeves when not in use.

Boxes of blank floppy disks come with a packet of adhesive labels. If you're using 5¼-inch floppies, however, avoid writing on them once you've stuck them onto the disk. If you must write on a label that has already been stuck on the disk, use a soft-tipped pen.

Do not bend floppies. Hold them only by the edges, never touching the shiny parts. Keep magnets away from them. Don't store them where they can get wet or expose them to temperatures below 50°F or above 125°F.

■ *Protect your system from dust, smoke, and static electricity.* These contaminants can do a surprising amount of damage if allowed to accumulate. Keep the

PERSONAL
COMPUTERS
FOR THE
COMPUTER
ILLITERATE

152

CPU, monitor, keyboard, and printer covered when not in use. (Dust covers are widely available from computer product dealers and office supply outlets.) Never, however, leave any component covered while the power is on or you'll risk overheating the system. Clean hardware and the area around hardware by vacuuming rather than dusting or sweeping. But vacuum gently, preferably with a hand-held unit, and only when the system is turned off.

Over time, exposure to smoke can damage your system. That is, your PC system. It can really gum up the works. So if you smoke while working at your PC, open the window or set up a little fan to blow the smoke yonder, away from your expensive, dependent hardware.

Static electricity can disrupt normal operations and zap stored data. You can minimize your system's potential exposure to static electricity by not operating electric motors nearby, by increasing humidity in the room, by avoiding materials (synthetic carpets and clothing, for example) subject to static buildup. Special products like antistatic floorpads, chairs, and sprays are also widely available.

- *Extend the life of your monitor by turning the brightness control all the way down when you expect to be away from your PC for more than a few minutes.* Better yet, get yourself a "screen blanker" utility, software that automatically blacks out the monitor when it's turned on but not in use. The utility reactivates the screen when you touch the mouse or strike any key.

- *Extend the life of your vision by eliminating glare on the screen and adjusting the brightness of the display to a level you find comfortable (look for the knob on the front, top, side, or on the back of the monitor).* Many authorities advise working in a darkened room, although some users find this uncomfortable. Antiglare filters are available from most general computer products stores or from direct marketing suppliers. Also, if your vision is weak to begin with, ask about magnification screens or utilities that automatically enlarge display type on the screen. Finally, rest your eyes every few minutes by closing them or casting your gaze elsewhere.

- *Encourage young children, even toddlers, to explore your personal computer and learn to use it, but only under adult supervision.* The last thing you want is peanut butter in your floppy drives or to discover that your data have been erased by a happy, squealing child or—

eek!—to find your mouse, severed tail and all, in the busy hands of a sandbox engineer burrowing through little kid-made hillocks as you weep.

■ *Practice good housekeeping with your data files and directories.* If you start creating files and directories— also called folders—helter-skelter with no overall sense of organization, they can quickly become a confusing, unproductive mess. Some people, I know, have an incredibly difficult time with the concept of good organization. To paraphrase Lincoln, I think they lack that bump. But please try; believe me, good organization will save you much grief.

How do you practice good housekeeping? Much the same as you do with paper files and folders in conventional file cabinets, by viewing your data as parts of a whole rather than as sovereign, disconnected entities. In other words, be consistent in how you name files and directories. Create one system and stick with it. If, for example, you organize client directories by name of client, avoid switching to a new system whereby you store client files by city or by the type of work involved or some other scheme. Think ahead and plan accordingly.

There are, incidentally, any number of software utilities and applications available under the general headings, "file management" or "hard disk management." These can help you organize and reorganize your data or help you find "misplaced" data, among other things.

**PERSONAL
COMPUTERS
FOR THE
COMPUTER
ILLITERATE**

154

• *Save data often.* Just do it! Get in the habit from day one. (You wouldn't have to be told if you had heard the anguished data loss screams I've heard, including my own.) Further, never, I mean *never ever*, get up from working at your PC without saving first. Never, do you hear? Not even to walk across the room to flip the cassette in the stereo. There's simply no way you or anyone can know when the power might fail or when you or some kid or four-legged friend is going to trip over the electrical cord feeding your PC.

• *Make backups of absolutely everything.* When you bring a new application home and copy it onto your hard disk, put the original disks away for safekeeping. These backups are insurance, replacements in case something happens to your working copies. You should keep current backups for all your data. This becomes a chore only if you fail to do it routinely.

Like most people with hard disks, I keep all my master applications and files on the hard disk. For backups I keep floppies that parallel my directories. Whenever I'm working in a particular directory I stick the corresponding floppy in one of the disk drives. Every time I save my work to the hard disk, I also save it to the floppy. Nice 'n' easy. Safe. Smart.

• *Buy a file recovery utility.* This is really a must because it's surprisingly easy to erase electronic files, including backups, by accident. A file recovery program allows you to "unerase" files, restoring them to health in your hard disk or on a floppy. You may not need it often, but just one use can easily justify its cost.

■ *Beware of floppy disk incompatibilities.* All floppy disks are not the same. The most obvious difference is size. A 3½-inch disk won't work in a 5¼-inch drive and vice versa. Other differences are more subtle. Some floppy disks, for example, have higher *densities* than others, allowing more data to be stored. The problem is, a low-density floppy disk drive cannot read high-density disks (though a high-density drive can usually read a low-density disk). Similar incompatibilities are cropping up as floppy disk technology advances (the perennial goal is to cram more data in the same or a smaller space). Ask your dealer or guru about these.

■ *Sit in a comfortable chair.* You have to admit, it makes zero sense to spare your system but spoil your spine. So sit up, take notice, and take care of your back.

AN OUNCE
OF
PREVENTION
AND SIMPLE
CURES: TIPS
FOR NEW
USERS

155

**PERSONAL
COMPUTERS
FOR THE
COMPUTER
ILLITERATE**

156

- *If you're worried about electromagnetic radiation
from your monitor (often called VDT—video display terminal—radiation), ask your dealer about a radiation filter.* Should you be worried? My personal disposition
about environmental and occupational concerns is to err
on the side of caution. Yet I don't use a radiation filter
myself. This is a big and growing issue, but as yet, there's
no agreement about the possible harmful effects of long-
term exposure to low-frequency radiation. (By the way,
this form of radiation is very common in our lives; micro-
wave ovens, power transmission lines, electric blankets,
and many other common sources have been identified as
sources of electromagnetic radiation.)

- *If you're concerned about power spikes and surges,
you can buy a power strip with a built-in surge protector.*
Should you worry? Not necessarily. Surges destructive
enough to do physical damage to your hardware are rare.
And most central processing units come with limited
built-in protection. Power strips designed to sacrifice
their lives in defense of your PC (or anything else plugged
into them), however, are usually inexpensive. They also
help you tame the Medusa-like tangle of cords that always seem to proliferate when you bring a PC home or
to the office. If you use a surge protector, be sure to plug
all your PC components into it, not just the CPU. And be
sure your system is completely grounded: Put all three-
pronged plugs into three-pronged outlets, using adapters
if necessary. If you do use an adapter, ask your dealer or
someone at your local hardware store how to make sure
it's grounded as well.

- *You can protect your system against theft and other
calamities.* Ask your dealer about hardware locks and
cables. If you have a homeowner's policy or equivalent
insurance, don't assume that it covers your PC and related components or every conceivable situation. All insurance coverage is not equal. Some policies reimburse
for purchase price, others for current value, still others
for replacement costs. One policy may protect hardware
but not software (which often represents the greater investment). Insuring data—which is, after all, your work
—is not always possible. Check with your agent. No matter how well you're insured, take precautions yourself:
Always make backups and store them in a separate place.

DEALING WITH TROUBLE

AN OUNCE
OF
PREVENTION
AND SIMPLE
CURES: TIPS
FOR NEW
USERS

157

Whenever I ask my friend P. if I can confide in her, P. always laughs and then replies, "Don't worry, your secret won't be safe with me." This in turn makes me laugh, for P. is right, there really is no need to worry when you know the outcome. I mention this because I must bear similar tidings to you: Don't worry, your PC will break down.

Well, it won't *break down* necessarily, but sooner or later it definitely will stop working the way you expect it to. It will stall. It will go blank. It will bring unwanted mystery into your life.

What do you do when this happens? I can't say; there are far too many possible explanations. But I do know that you can save time, money, and worry by checking for common ailments before calling the technician.

■ *When your system or any component goes down, check cables, connections, switches, plugs, knobs, and dials before hitting the Panic Button.* I can't tell you how many times I've seen my screen go blank or watched it go suddenly monochrome (I have a color monitor) or heard the sickening down-gear sound of electrical power draining from the system. Only to discover, upon a ridiculously cursory inspection, that a cable has come unscrewed or that my independently minded, ever-probing foot has teased the power cord out of the power strip. Sometimes you'll discover that everything's plugged in all right, but the whole room or building or neighborhood is suffering a power failure. Check this out before jumping out the window (or throwing your PC out the window).

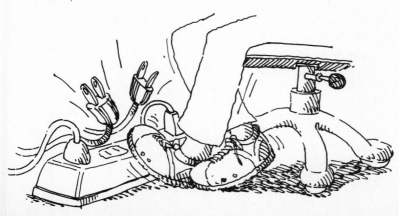

**PERSONAL
COMPUTERS
FOR THE
COMPUTER
ILLITERATE**

158

■ *Start from scratch.* That's right, when your PC seizes up or hits some perplexing snag, simply hit the reset button if you have one. If not, shut the system down by flipping off the power switch, wait half a minute (never flip it off and right on again), and power up.

■ *If you have access to a compatible machine, try using your application on it.* At the very least this can help you determine whether you've got a hardware problem or a software problem.

■ *Check your manual before calling your personal guru or the technician.* If you're like many, perhaps most, users you wouldn't think of condescending to look for a solution in your manual (system software manual, personal computer manual, printer manual, whatever), at least not until the technician asks if you've checked the manual. Save the technician the trouble: Check the manual first.

■ *When all else fails, call your guru, your dealer, the manufacturer (some manufacturers provide technical assistance phone numbers), or your religious counselor.* Good luck.

8

ANTIDOTES TO PC ILLITERACY: INDEX, GLOSSARY, AND ENLIGHTENMENT . . . IN PLAIN ENGLISH

Illiterate? Write Now for Free Help.
—SOPHOMORIC BUT FUNNY BUMPER STICKER SPOTTED IN COLLEGE DORM

ACCESSORIES. *See* FURNITURE/ACCESSORIES.

ACCOUNTING SOFTWARE. A natural application category for personal computers—because PCs are so well suited to automating accounts receivable, accounts payable, etc. *See* page 53.

ADAPTER BOARD. *See* ENHANCEMENT BOARD.

ADD-IN BOARD. *See* ENHANCEMENT BOARD.

ADD-IN SOFTWARE. *See* page 63.

ALTAIR. The first personal computer, sold in kit form, introduced in the mid-1970s and credited with inspiring Steve Jobs and Steve Wozniak, the founders of Apple Computer, and advancing the careers of Paul Allen and Bill Gates, founders of Microsoft, the largest supplier of personal computer software in the world. *See also* COMPUTER CELEBRITIES (MODERN ERA).

AMIGA. *See* COMMODORE AMIGA

APPLE II COMPUTER. A line of small, relatively inexpensive personal computers used mainly in homes and schools; *see* page 127.

APPLE MACINTOSH. A line of innovative personal computers that emphasize simplicity and ease of use without sacrificing power and flexibility. *See* page 121.

APPLICATION PROGRAM. When you buy a PC application, you're buying a finished product, an invisible set of electronic instructions that convert your PC from a dust-collecting conversation piece to a specialized machine. Applications give personal computers purpose, a raison d'être—a reason to be. You use different applications on the same PC to write,

PERSONAL
COMPUTERS
FOR THE
COMPUTER
ILLITERATE

160

create images, calculate, send and receive messages—to do all kinds of tasks.

ARTIFICIAL INTELLIGENCE (AI). Computer *reasoning*, in contrast to *processing*. Most observers consider artificial intelligence an interesting but still elusive goal, at least for PC-based applications. Still, you're likely to *see* "Contains Artificial Intelligence!" emblazoned in bold letters on some applications ads and packages. Such claims should be greeted with a healthy dose of skepticism.

ASCII (AMERICAN STANDARD CODE FOR INFORMATION EXCHANGE). Personal computers can process only numerical information. They don't understand words and letters. ASCII (always pronounced "askee" rather than by individual letters) is a widely used system in which letters of the alphabet, punctuation marks, common symbols (percent sign, asterisk, pound sign, etc.), and other nonnumerical data are represented by numbers. For example, the letter *A* is represented by the number 65.

AT. Short for "Advanced Technology," a common name for IBM PCs and IBM PC-compatibles employing the Intel 80286 microprocessor. Pronounce the initials: ay-tee. *See* page 118.

BACKPLANE. The portion of the central processing unit into which you can plug enhancement boards. In most personal computers, the backplane is located on the mother board.

BACKUP. A backup is an extra copy of software, whether applications (working software) or data (the work you create using applications). Imagine that I'm grabbing you by the shoulders and shaking you vigorously. At the same time, I'm practically shouting: "Backups are very important! You'd better know about backups!" To understand why, *see* pages 74 and 154.

BATCH FILE. To make applications work you execute commands, usually by striking designated keys on the keyboard or pointing and clicking with a computer mouse. Sometimes you have to execute a series of individual commands, one after another, to make the application do what you want. Intermediate and advanced users commonly automate series of commands by creating batch files. This allows them to execute the entire series by executing a single command.

BAUD RATE. *See* BITS PER SECTION.

BIG BLUE. Common nickname for International Business Machines, Inc., inspired by the blue suits IBM salesmen wore almost exclusively for many years or by the color of paint traditionally used on IBM mainframe computers.

BINARY CODE. When you give your personal computer a PRINT command, it doesn't recognize the word "print." Instead, the command is transmitted as a series of on and off signals arranged in a pattern, or code, that means print.

Ultimately, all user commands, applications, data, and other forms of computer software are nothing more than on and off signals. The on signals are faint electrical impulses. The off signals are nothing; they're the absence of impulses. By arranging these on and off signals in patterns, programmers create computer instructions—software. Since the instruction code consists of only two kinds of information, on and off, it's called binary code or binary instruction (bi = two). To represent the code, programmers use the number 1 for on signals and 0 for off.

This is a lot like another famous binary system, Morse code, except that Morse code uses long and short signals instead of on and off impulses. For example, in Morse code, the standard signal for distress, SOS, is denoted by three short signals followed by three long signals followed by three short signals:

beep-beep-beep

beeeeep-beeeeep-beeeeep

beep-beep-beep

Morse code uses dots and bars to represent short and long signals. SOS looks like this:

● ● ● - - - ● ● ●

If you substituted 0's for short beeps and 1's for long beeps, SOS would look like this:

000111000

As you might have guessed, whether you're using long-and-short or on-and-off signals, you can create an infinite number of codes—instructions—by arranging the two simple binary elements in different ways. This is the secret of all computers. This is also why they're called digital machines, since they work by converting information to digits, 1's and 0's.

Each binary element, the 1's and 0's (on and off pulses) is called a bit. Computers are designed to read bits in groups of eight. These groups are called bytes.

BIT. *See* BINARY CODE.

BITS PER SECOND (BPS). A measure of speed, not unlike miles per hour, except that instead of measuring how fast a car is cruising the interstate, bits per second measures the rate at which modems (communications hardware) transmit and receive data over phone lines. *See* page 101.

BOOTING UP. The process of turning on a personal computer and activating its system software. *See* page 10.

BPS. *See* BITS PER SECOND.

BUFFER. A buffer is a temporary storage place for software, usually data. Many printers and other peripheral hardware devices come with software buffers. Here's how they work. Let's say you want to print a long file, a thirty-page report. If your printer prints at a rate of six pages per minute (ppm), it will need five minutes to do the job. You've got lots of work to do; the last thing you need is to have your PC tied up for five minutes printing your report. Fortunately, this isn't necessary. For when you execute the PRINT command, the file is

ANTIDOTES
TO PC
ILLITERACY:
INDEX,
GLOSSARY,
AND
ENLIGHTENMENT
...IN PLAIN
ENGLISH

161

PERSONAL
COMPUTERS
FOR THE
COMPUTER
ILLITERATE

162

automatically transmitted to the printer buffer, freeing your machine for other work.

The word "buffer" has taken on a more general meaning among many PC users. If you're trying to give an obviously harried colleague important information, for example, you could say, "Put that in your buffer and get back to me," meaning "I can see you're busy so think about it when you have a minute and let me know what you decide." Or the colleague might say, "Let me buffer that for a minute; I'll get back to you."

BUG/BUGGY. A bug is simply a glitch. There are hardware bugs and software bugs. *See* pages 73 and 142.

BUILDING YOUR OWN PC. A surprisingly accessible challenge that appeals mainly to wires-and-pliers types. *See* page 144.

BULLETIN BOARD. *See* ELECTRONIC BULLETIN BOARD.

BUS. The internal electronic instruction and data pathways— wires, circuits, and all that jazz—of personal computers.

BUYING PCS AND PC PRODUCTS. *See* page 131.

BYTE. *See* BINARY CODE.

CAD. *See* COMPUTER-AIDED DESIGN.

CARD. *See* ENHANCEMENT BOARD.

CATHODE RAY TUBE (CRT). *See* MONITOR.

CD-ROM. Properly equipped, personal computers can use compact disks that look exactly like the audio CDs. PC CDs are called CD-ROMs (Compact Disk Read-Only Memory) or ROM disks. Instead of storing music, they store applications, data, still and moving images, and audio, including . . . music. You need a peripheral device called a CD-ROM drive in order to use ROM disks. *See* pages 44 and 102.

CD-ROM DRIVE. *See* CD-ROM.

CENTRAL PROCESSING UNIT (CPU). The computer's brain, the computing part of a personal computer, the hardware component, in other words, responsible for running the show, doing what needs to be done, dealing the cards, getting out the vote, and shaping up the troops. *See* pages 12 and 78.

CHARACTERS PER SECOND (CPS). One way to measure the speed of a printer. Another way is pages per minute (PPM). *See* page 93.

CHASSIS. The cabinet or box enclosing the central processing unit, printer, or other type of PC hardware.

CLONE. Originally, clone referred to personal computers that were, functionally at least, copies of higher-priced IBM PCs. These were IBM PC "work-alikes." When companies started introducing new models that improved on the IBM PC standard, the word "clone" began to seem inappropriate because these machines were, more often than not, mere copies. Today, the words "clone" and "compatible" are used more or less interchangeably.

COMMAND. A computer command is the same as a human command. Do this! Do that! The method of communicating commands to computers, however, is different. *See* page 14.

COMMODORE AMIGA.   A personal computer with strong graphics capabilities often purchased for use at home. *See page 128.*

COMMUNICATIONS.   An important PC application. *See page 40.*

COMPATIBILITY.   Compatibility has several meanings in the realm of personal computers. *See* CLONE and *see* pages 70 and 109.

COMPUTER-AIDED DESIGN (CAD).   An application used mainly by architects, drafters, engineers, and designers that augments or replaces traditional mechanical methods of drawing floor plans, elevations, technical illustrations, schemata, and other professional renderings. *See page 61.*

COMPUTER CELEBRITIES (HISTORICAL).   One thing you may notice if you hang around veteran PC users for very long is that they seem to know a lot about certain dead people with some connection to the history of computer science. Actually, they don't know much at all. Read the following brief bios, and you'll join the PC cognoscenti. Amaze your friends. Impress strangers. Become an instant veteran. Read on.

John Napier, a Scottish mathematician born in 1550 gets credit for inventing—discovering—logarithms. You know, exponents, those little numbers that hover at shoulder height just to the right of regular numbers. In 2^3 (or $2 \times 2 \times 2$), for example, 2 is the base number and ^{3} is the logarithm. Logarithms are important to computers because they streamline mathematical computations. Napier's 1614 invention, "Napier's Bones," a set of sticks etched with numerals, greatly advanced calculating technology.

Building on the work of others before him, English mathematician *William Oughtred* invented the slide rule in 1630.

Few lights shine brighter in the long history of computing than that of the Frenchman, *Blaise Pascal.* In 1642, Pascal, then just nineteen, designed a practical desktop adding machine composed of interconnected wheels marked with the numerals 0 to 9. Pascal was inspired by the sight of his father, a tax official, slaving day after day over bleak, repetitive computations. Pascal's invention, called the Pascaline, was the forerunner of mechanical adding machines, which prevailed until introduction of the electronic calculator. Pascal's contributions are honored today by a computer language bearing his name.

Once upon a time in America, a couple of decades ago, a great army (of women, mostly) labored as "key punch operators." What a key punch operator did all day was transfer written information from questionnaires and other forms to key punch cards, uniform pieces of stiff paper perforated with tiny, usually rectangular holes in various arrangements. The cards were fed into monstrous mainframe computers that gobbled up the information represented by the holes. While mainframes were a post–World War II invention, key punch cards harken to the earliest years of the nineteenth century when a French silk weaver by the name of *Joseph Marie Jac-*

PERSONAL
COMPUTERS
FOR THE
COMPUTER
ILLITERATE

164

quard invented them to control skeins of silk in commercial looms. The Jacquard loom was hailed as a miracle and its inventor, a hero of France. Little did M. Jacquard know that someday he would be hailed as a hero of computer science as well.

No one contributed more to the actual design of a practical computer in the early nineteenth century than the zealous English mathematician, *Charles Babbage*. The problem was, Babbage was decades ahead of his time. The technology for actually building a working model of his designs lagged far behind his ability to imagine and design the contraptions. This hardly discouraged the man from trying, though. His first effort, subsidized by the government, was called the Difference Machine. It was ultimately built by a Swedish printer. Babbage's second great inspiration, the Analytical Engine, though never built, greatly influenced those who followed.

Few contemporaries contributed as much to the development of Charles Babbage's ideas as his dear friend, the brilliant mathematician *Augusta Ada Byron*, Countess of Lovelace, and daughter of the Romantic poet Lord Byron. Lovelace "seems to understand the Analytical Engine better than I do, and is far, far better at explaining it," Babbage wrote. Lovelace also laid much of the groundwork for today's computer programmers. The computer language, Ada, was named in honor of her memory.

Boolean algebra (or Boolean logic) seems to excite advanced computer types more than anything else in life, more even than the privilege of getting to choose the toppings for a shared pizza. And well it ought to, for Boolean algebra, all but useless in its own time, provides the basis for logic design in modern computers, including PCs. Without logic, computers are little more than TVs with bad reception. The man behind Boolean logic is *George Boole*, an English mathematician whose lofty works include a book with one of the nineteenth century's great titles, *An Investigation of the Laws of Thought*.

COMPUTER CELEBRITIES (MODERN ERA). *Herman Hollerith*, the U.S.-born son of German immigrants, kicked off the modern era of computers with a statistical tabulator he invented to streamline the 1890 census. Incorporating an idea first proposed by Charles Babbage, Hollerith's tabulator employed punched cards to count raw data—occupation, country of birth, sex, age, number of children, and so forth—collected by census takers. Boosted by his great success, Hollerith formed a company called the Tabulating Machine Company, currently known as International Business Machines, Inc., IBM for short.

By World War II, *Thomas Watson, Sr.*, had built IBM into a leading manufacturer of typewriters, tabulators, mechanical calculators, and . . . grocery scales. Watson imbued his employees with pious exhortations, hanging huge banners in prominent places urging them to THINK. His commitment to research and development of more sophisticated data processors was propelled by America's entry into World War II and by his postwar determination to lead the field.

Englishman *Alan Turing* was a brilliant and eccentric gay mathematician widely credited with designing the code-breaking computer, dubbed Colossus, that helped the Allies defeat Nazi Germany. He later helped develop the Automatic Computer Engine (ACE), one of the first machines to employ stored programs.

At the end of World War II, Hungarian-born *John von Neumann* laid down the design principles of modern mainframes (and personal computers) in a key memorandum. His influence on the future direction of computer technology was so great that for many years computer scientists referred to mainframes as von Neumann machines.

Grace Hopper is best known for popularizing the term *debugging* after she and her colleagues discovered a dead moth in the Mark I, a huge mechanical World War II vintage computer. More significantly, Hopper was a software and computer language specialist who made critical contributions to development of UNIVAC I, the first commercial mainframe computer.

Steve Jobs and *Steve Wozniak*—"the Two Steves," as they're often called—founded Apple Computer in the late seventies while in their early twenties. Their success kicked off a period of spectacular innovation in the small machines we call personal computers. *See* page 127.

Bill Gates, another in a long tradition of ridiculously young movers and shakers, cofounded Microsoft Corporation (with Paul Allen) in the mid-1970s to market their version of BASIC, a popular computer language. Microsoft's fortunes blossomed wildly when IBM chose its version of DOS as the standard operating system for the IBM PC.

COMPUTER LANGUAGE. All applications are actually sets of coded instructions. These instructions are written by PC users and professional application developers (called "programmers") using one or more of many available sets of formal notation. Such rules and standards are called computer languages. *See* page 75.

CONNECTIVITY. A buzzword that, like most buzzwords (including "buzzword"), gets lots of play but lacks precision. Most people who use *connectivity* seem to be referring to local area networks (LANS), PC communications, or both.

CONTEXT-SENSITIVE HELP. *See* ON-SCREEN HELP.

COPROCESSOR. A kind of performance booster for certain PC applications, such as electronic spreadsheets and computer aided design (CAD). *See* page 79.

COPY PROTECTION. The exceedingly unpopular and increasingly rare practice of preventing consumers from making copies (illegal or otherwise) of commercial applications. Where it

PERSONAL
COMPUTERS
FOR THE
COMPUTER
ILLITERATE

166

exists, copy protection is built into the application. *See* page 74.

CPS. *See* CHARACTERS PER SECOND.

CPU. *See* CENTRAL PROCESSING UNIT.

CRASH. In computer lingo, a synonym for "fail," as in "My hard disk crashed yesterday and I've decided to kill myself."

CRT. *See* MONITOR.

CURSOR/POINTER. The movable flashing rectangle, arrow, or other type of shape on an active personal computer monitor. *See* page 15.

DAISY WHEEL PRINTER. A noisy contraption that can't print graphics. *See* page 99.

DATA. The text, graphics, numbers, and other information you create or manipulate with applications are called *data*. Applications, in other words, do the work; data *are* the work. (The word "data," by the way, is the plural of datum, so if you want to be grammatically correct you should say, "these data are," instead of "this data is." Be warned, however, the Anglophone world drifts elsewhere: Making verbs and pronouns agree with the plural "data" will place you in a tiny minority of English speakers.) *See* page 10.

DATABASE MANAGEMENT SYSTEM (DBMS). One of the traditional "Big Three" PC applications (along with electronic spreadsheets and word processors). Databases are used to file, search, retrieve, and mix and match human, scientific, government, corporate, in short, all kinds of data. *See* page 36.

DAUGHTER BOARD. *See* ENHANCEMENT BOARD.

DBMS. *See* DATABASE MANAGEMENT SYSTEM.

DEDICATED MACHINE. Dedicated means specialized. A dedicated machine is one that specializes in a particular function, like a waffle iron or copy machine. A machine that can only do word processing is a dedicated word processor. Personal computers are not dedicated machines since you can use them to do many different kinds of things—including word processing. *See* page 5.

DEFAULT. If you give a dinner party on the second Saturday of every month and *always* invite your neighbors, Chris and Pat, you could say that Chris and Pat are *default* guests. That is, unless you inform them otherwise, they automatically assume they are invited. PCs, system software, applications, and hardware peripherals also employ the default principle. They make certain assumptions—that you want to work from your hard drive rather than from a floppy drive, for example —unless you instruct them otherwise.

DEMONSTRATION DISKS. *See* page 140.

DENSITY. *See* page 155.

DESKTOP PUBLISHING (DPT). A professional and personal application for using PC in graphic design. *See* page 51.

DIGITAL. *See* BINARY CODE.

DIRECTORY. *See* FILE, FOLDER, AND DIRECTORY.

DISCOUNTS. The conventional wisdom is no different when it comes to PC hardware and software: Never pay list price. *See* page 141.

DISKETTE. *See* FLOPPY DISK.

DOCUMENTATION. Operating instructions for PC hardware and software. *See* page 67.

DOS. Disk operating system, the principle system software for IBM PCs, PC compatibles, and IBM PS machines. DOS is the single-most popular system software for personal computers in the world. *See* page 117.

DO'S AND DON'TS. *See* page 149.

DOT MATRIX PRINTER. The most common—and generally least expensive—type of personal computer printer. It generates tiny dots on a page that form text or graphics. *See* page 97.

DOTS PER INCH (DPI). The standard measure of printer quality. *See* page 93.

DPI. *See* DOTS PER INCH.

DRAW PROGRAM. *See* FREEHAND PAINT AND DRAW PROGRAMS.

DTP. *See* DESKTOP PUBLISHING.

EASE OF USE. An important, if elusive, consideration when selecting hardware and software. *See* pages 67 and 93.

8088, 8086, 80286, 80386. *See* MICROPROCESSOR.

EISA. *See* MICROCHANNEL ARCHITECTURE.

ELECTRONIC BULLETIN BOARD. The computer version of conventional wall-mounted bulletin boards. You view announcements and messages on an electronic bulletin board on your monitor after gaining access to it via phone lines. You can also "tack up" your own announcements and messages for other PC users to view. *See* page 41.

ELECTRONIC MAIL (E-MAIL). E-Mail is a service that allows you to turn your PC into an electronic mailbox. You can send and receive text and other kinds of data almost instantaneously. *See* page 40.

ELECTRONIC SPREADSHEET. One of the traditional "Big Three" PC applications (along with database management systems and word processing). Electronic spreadsheets are commonly used by businesspeople, accountants, researchers, and many others to make multiple calculations almost instantly. The introduction of a fast, versatile electronic spreadsheet, Lotus 1-2-3, in 1982, is often credited with attracting big business to personal computers. *See* page 38.

E-MAIL. *See* ELECTRONIC MAIL.

ENHANCEMENT BOARD. A hardware component that fits inside the central processing unit, enhancing the PC's capabilities. *See* page 80.

ENTERTAINMENT SOFTWARE. There are hundreds, more likely thousands, of PC-based games, puzzles, and other amusements, ranging from the ingenious and appealing to the asinine. *See* page 32.

EXPANSION BOARD. *See* ENHANCEMENT BOARD.

EXTENDED INDUSTRY STANDARD ARCHITECTURE (EISA). *See* MICROCHANNEL ARCHITECTURE.

PERSONAL
COMPUTERS
FOR THE
COMPUTER
ILLITERATE

168

FILE, FOLDER, AND DIRECTORY. A file is the basic organizational unit for the work you create—the data you save—with a PC. If you want to write a letter to the city protesting a plan to cut down a beloved shade tree on your block, for example, you first create an electronic file and give it a file name. I would call this one "Tree." When you're finished writing the letter, you can print a copy of it and then store it on your hard disk or floppy (or both). Its file name allows you to retrieve it later, if desired.

You can create electronic folders, or directories as they're also called, for storing related files. If you write lots of protest letters, you may want to create a folder called "Protest Letters," for example, for storing "Tree" and other gadfly screeds, missives, and epistles.

Personal computers allow you to extend this organizational scheme indefinitely by creating folders within folders. For example, if you write personal letters, business letters, and letters related to a book you're researching, as well as protest letters, you can create separate electronic folders for each group. But you can also create a master folder labeled "Correspondence."

This system of electronic organization mimics conventional filing systems that use manila files, hanging folders, partitions, drawers, and filing cabinets. PC users employ this scheme for the same reason people use conventional files, folders, etc.: to make it easy to find what you're looking for, even years after storing it.

FILE RECOVERY PROGRAM. Everybody inadvertently loses electronic files from time to time. That's why everybody should have access to a file recovery program, a software utility that can often restore lost computer files. *See* page 64.

FIXED DISK. *See* HARD DISK.

FLOPPY DISK. The PC's version of audiocassettes, which is to say a portable medium for storing applications, data, and other forms of software. *See* pages 11 and 81.

FLOPPY DISK CARE. *See* page 150.

FLOPPY DISK DRIVE. The PC hardware unit that reads portable software (floppy disks). *See* pages 13 and 82.

FOLDER. *See* FILE, FOLDER, AND DIRECTORY.

FOOTPRINT. The space required on a desktop or other surface for a PC or other hardware component. Not surprisingly, small footprints are all the rage.

FORMATTING. Before you can use a new blank floppy disk, you have to prepare it in a simple procedure called formatting, sometimes called "initializing." When you give your PC a command to format a blank floppy disk, what you're really doing is electronically organizing the floppy in such a way that you can store and retrieve applications or data on it effortlessly.

486 PC. *See* MICROPROCESSOR.

FREEHAND DRAW AND PAINT PROGRAMS. Graphics applications that allow you to turn your PC into a sketch pad or canvas. *See* page 48.

FURNITURE/ACCESSORIES.   *See* page 104.

GAMES.   *See* ENTERTAINMENT.

GIGO.   Garbage In Garbage Out (pronounced JEE-go), an important principle in personal computing, not to mention life at large. The basic idea here is that if your input is garbage, your output will be garbage, another way of saying, you get out of something what you put into it. Think of word processors. Most people, including professional writers, who discover word processors are instant converts. *"Viva* Word Processing!" writers proclaim. And with good reason. It's wonderful, liberating even, to be able to move blocks of copy around in the bat of an eyelash or to correct the spelling of "accomodation" (two *m*'s: accommodation) throughout a fifty-page article with a single keystroke. But word processors don't write; writers write. Word processors are merely tools. Bad writers do not become good writers simply because they abandon their pencils for word processors. If their ideas and language structure and style are garbage, their writing will be garbage, even if written with a word processor. Same with everything else you can do with a PC. Same with life: You can't make a silk purse out of a sow's ear. Garbage in garbage out. GIGO.

GRAPHICAL USER INTERFACE (GUI).   Applications in which commands and other elements are represented by little pictures called icons or by words arranged in lists called pulldown menus are said to have a graphical user interface. The Mac's graphical user interface has had a great influence on interface design for other PC systems. *See* page 110.

GRAPHICS.   A broad and extremely varied application category. Graphics products range from expensive, rarefied programs for artists, illustrators, and other professionals to business-oriented graphics programs to easily mastered, useful, and fun programs for nonartists and children. *See* page 47.

GUI.   *See* GRAPHICAL USER INTERFACE.

HACKER.   A computer enthusiast.

HARD COPY.   When users print work they've created on the PC, they often call it hard copy to distinguish it from text or graphics that remain stored as software in the system.

HARD DISK.   A hardware component used for electronically storing system software, applications, data—any kind of PC software. Hard disks are considered *mass* storage devices because their capacity is much greater than that of a floppy disk. Once considered a luxury, hard disks are increasingly viewed as a necessity. *See* page 81.

HARDWARE.   The central processing unit, monitor, keyboard, mouse, printer, and other hard, heavy, bulky components of a personal computer; anything that's not software. *See* pages 8, 12, and 76.

HELP LINE.   Telephone-based technical or operational assistance; *see* page 73.

**PERSONAL
COMPUTERS
FOR THE
COMPUTER
ILLITERATE**

170

HOUSEKEEPING. The practice of keeping computer files well organized. *See* page 153.

IBM PC AND IBM PC-COMPATIBLES. *See* page 117.

IBM PS SERIES. The line of IBM personal computers that replaced the original IBM PC line. *See* page 124.

ICON. In system software and applications, a little picture representing a command or system component. *See* GRAPHICAL USER INTERFACE.

INK JET PRINTER. A kind of printer that sprays ink on the page. *See* page 99.

INOCULATION. *See* VIRUS.

INPUT DEVICE. Any hardware component—the keyboard and mouse, for example—used to execute commands in applications or create data. *See* pages 14 and 85–91.

INSTALL. A common verb in this business, one whose meaning is nearly the same as for other kinds of products. When you buy a new application, you usually have to *install* it. This one-time procedure is usually a matter of slipping the application floppy disks into an active floppy drive and executing a few commands as instructed by the manual (or by on-screen messages generated by the new application itself).

INTEGRATED APPLICATION Several applications—word processing, electronic spreadsheet, database management system, and communications, for example—rolled into one software product. *See* page 28.

INTEGRATED CIRCUIT. *See* MICROCHIP.

INTERACTIVE. A silly but very common adjective that has come to mean little more than "engaging." An interactive application is one that engages you, or at least appears to engage you, not only prompting you for responses but seeming to react to your responses in original ways. A product that claims to be 100 percent interactive is not unlike a person claiming to be 100 percent air-breathing. PC applications are inherently interactive since it takes two, user and machine, to tango.

INTERFACE. The boundary between a machine and its human user. In cars, dashboards are the interface. On VCRs, the interface is the control panel. On personal computers, an application's interface is what appears on the monitor and how the application makes use of input devices to execute commands. *See* page 110.

JAGGIES. An undesirable, but sometimes unavoidable stair-step effect common in the diagonal lines or curves of graphics generated by some PC printers, especially dot matrix printers.

JARGON. The world is full of self-important people of limited scope and diminished intellect whose idea of progress is to substitute constipated new words for immediately recognizable, enlightening ones. Unfortunately, the PC industry has more than its fair share of these slope-headed bludgeon-tongued lingo-cretins. Their unwelcome creations are called jargon, an ancient word rooted in the Sanskrit *gharghara-h*—what we call "gurgling."

ANTIDOTES
TO PC
ILLITERACY:
INDEX,
GLOSSARY,
AND
ENLIGHTENMENT
... IN PLAIN
ENGLISH

171

JOYSTICK. A kind of input device used primarily to control PC-based action games. *See* page 89.

KEYBOARD. The most common and versatile PC input device. *See* pages 14 and 85.

KILOBYTE. Approximately 1000 bytes (1024 bytes, to be exact).

LAN. *See* LOCAL AREA NETWORK.

LANGUAGE. *See* COMPUTER LANGUAGE.

LAPTOP COMPUTER. A compact (or relatively compact), lightweight (or relatively lightweight) personal computer designed to be portable. Laptops weighing under six pounds are commonly called notebook computers. *See* page 112.

LASER PRINTER. The most popular and most affordable high-quality PC printer. *See* page 98.

LCD. *See* LIQUID CRYSTAL DISPLAY.

LED. *See* LIGHT-EMITTING DIODE.

LIGHT-EMITTING DIODE (LED). Jargon alert! A light-emitting diode is nothing more than a tiny display light, commonly used in control panels to indicate whether hardware is on (lighted) or off (not lighted), or whether something is currently active. "LED light" is a sloppy-minded redundancy.

LIGHT PEN. An uncommon input device. *See* page 89.

LIQUID CRYSTAL DISPLAY (LCD). A low-power, comparatively dim type of screen technology used on many portable and laptop personal computers.

LOCAL AREA NETWORK (LAN). Individual PCs linked by cables, allowing users to share applications and hardware and to communicate with each other. *See* pages 43 and 101.

LONG-TERM MEMORY. A vital facility of personal computers, allowing users to store applications, data, and other software indefinitely. The most common forms of long-term memory are floppy disks and hard disks, though CD-ROMs are becoming increasingly important.

LOTUS 1-2-3. The most famous, most popular, and most entrenched electronic spreadsheet, a giant among applications brand names, available mainly for machines that use DOS as their system software.

MACINTOSH. *See* APPLE MACINTOSH.

MAIL MERGE. An application used to prepare print runs for mailing labels, envelopes, customized salutations in form letters, and other elements of correspondence in mass mailings. *See* "Mass Mailing," page 23.

MAINFRAME COMPUTER. The big ones; with the exception of supercomputers, the most powerful and expensive class of computer. Mainframes are used mainly by governments, corporations, and well-endowed research institutions.

MANUAL. *See* DOCUMENTATION.

MASS STORAGE. Any device or medium that stores large amounts of software. Hard disks are mass storage devices. Others include removable cartridges, tape drives, and CD-ROMs.

MCA. *See* MICROCHANNEL ARCHITECTURE.

MEAN TIME BETWEEN FAILURE (MTBF). A standard rating for many kinds

PERSONAL
COMPUTERS
FOR THE
COMPUTER
ILLITERATE

172

of hardware. An MTBF rating of 5000 hours for a hard disk means that half of all hard disks of that type went kaput in laboratory tests before being used for 5000 hours and half did not. *See* page 144.

MEDIUM. A medium is neither one who leads seances nor the middle soft-drink-cup size at snack bars. Instead, it's the material on which software, usually applications and data, is stored electronically. Just as compact disks, cassette tape, and phonographs are *media* for musical recordings, the floppy disk is a *medium* for storing software applications and data. *See* "Using Applications," page 10.

MEGABYTE. Approximately one million bytes (exactly 1,048,576 bytes).

MEGAHERTZ (MHz). One million electrical cycles per second. Generally, the higher the megahertz rating of a personal computer, the greater its performance, which is to say, the faster it works. Most PCs process at between 8 and 20 MHz. Machines that process at a rate of over 20 MHz are generally considered high-performance models.

MEMORY. *See* LONG-TERM MEMORY, RANDOM ACCESS MEMORY, and READ-ONLY MEMORY.

MENU. A selection of commands in an application. *See* page 68.

MHz. *See* MEGAHERTZ.

MICROCHANNEL ARCHITECTURE (MCA). My stars and planets! The zillions of words that have been written about this . . . this . . . thing! All wildly contradictory. Microchannel architecture is a new bus—internal communication—technology featured in most models of IBM PS/2 computers (as well as some non-IBM machines under license to IBM). It is alleged by its maker to beef up performance and generate all kinds of wonderful benefits to users. Many quite respectable and certifiably independent critics not only question these claims, they scoff at them.

A number of IBM's competitors have banded together to offer an alternative to MCA called Extended Industry Standard Architecture, or EISA (rhymes with Lisa) for short. It is the opinion of many observers, me included, that neither MCA nor EISA has much relevancy for most users. The benefits, even if real and realizable, are the stuff of power users and computer professionals rather than professionals and others who use computers.

MICROCHIP. An integrated circuit, the fundamental building block of modern computers, and of many electronic goods. Microchips usually consist of silicon (refined sand) etched with hundreds of electrical pathways, resistors (oppose the flow of electricity), capacitors (store electrical charges), and transistors (amplify a charge or turn it off and on). Working together, these elements regulate the flow of electricity, the basis of information processing, or in a word, computing.

MICROCOMPUTER. Another way of saying personal computer.

MICROPROCESSOR. A kind of microchip, sometimes referred to as "a computer on a chip." A PC's microprocessor is responsible for calculations, processing, internal communications, and coordinating all the components of a PC system. Microprocessor manufacturers—the most prominent ones in the PC industry are Intel and Motorola—identify their products with numbers. The first IBM PCs and compatibles, for example, were built around Intel 8088 or 8086 microprocessors. Models introduced later used more advanced Intel 80286 and 80386 and 80486 microprocessors, usually identified by the last three digits only. All of these microprocessors are still in production. *See* page 79.

ANTIDOTES
TO PC
ILLITERACY:
INDEX,
GLOSSARY,
AND
ENLIGHTENMENT
... IN PLAIN
ENGLISH

173

MICROSOFT. The leading supplier of PC software, including DOS, the primary system software for IBM PCs, PC-compatibles, and IBM PS/2 machines.

MICROSOFT WINDOWS. A software product, technically termed an "operating environment," designed to give IBM PCs, IBM PC-compatibles, and IBM PS machines their own graphical user interface—to make them look and feel similar to an Apple Macintosh (though you can't run Mac applications on any of these machines). *See* page 110.

MIDI. Musical Instrument Digital Interface, a music-industry standard that helps assure playing compatability among electronic instruments. *See* page 55.

MINICOMPUTER. In the hierarchy of computers, there are personal computers, mainframes, supercomputers, and falling between PCs and mainframes, minicomputers.

MIPS. Millions of instructions per second. The processing speed of personal computers is often measured in MIPS.

MODEM. A peripheral hardware device used to connect PCs to standard phone lines, allowing users to exchange text and other forms of data near and far. *See* pages 40 and 100.

MONEY MANAGEMENT SOFTWARE. A vast class of related applications ranging from checkbook balancers to business management programs.

MONITOR. The part of the PC system that looks like a television set. Monitors are also called VDTs (video display terminals) and sometime CRTs (cathode ray tubes). *See* pages 10 and 11.

MONOCHROME. Single color (not necessarily the same as "black and white"). There are both monochrome monitors and color monitors.

MOTHER BOARD. The main circuit board inside the central processing unit. The mother board contains key components of the CPU, including the microprocessor.

MOUSE. An input device designed to be moved around by hand on a desktop. Its movement is mimicked on the screen. *See* pages 15 and 37.

MTBF. *See* MEAN TIME BETWEEN FAILURES.

MULTIMEDIA. An emerging application in which personal computers are used to produce and control audiovisual presentations. *See* page 57.

MULTIPROCESSING. Most personal computers can handle only one

PERSONAL
COMPUTERS
FOR THE
COMPUTER
ILLITERATE

174

application at a time. Advanced machines using sophisticated operating systems can run more than one application simultaneously. The ability is called multiprocessing. Few users really need this much computing power.

MUSIC. An important, though largely specialized application. *See* page 55.

MUSICAL INSTRUMENT DIGITAL INTERFACE. *See* MIDI.

NETWORK. *See* LOCAL AREA NETWORK.

NeXT COMPUTER. A personal computer designed by a relatively new company started by Steve Jobs, a founder of Apple Computer. *See* page 128.

NOTEBOOK COMPUTER. *See* LAPTOP COMPUTER.

NUMBER CRUNCHING. A colorful and popular term for computer-based calculating, especially the kind of calculating performed by spreadsheet applications. This is why electronic spreadsheets and the people who use them are often referred to as number crunchers.

OBSOLESCENCE. A widely misunderstood concept shamelessly exploited by many hardware and software companies, which are all too often more interested in increased sales than in truth. *See* page 141.

OCR. *See* OPTICAL CHARACTER READER.

ON-LINE SERVICES. You can do all kinds of things with a PC, a modem, and a communications program—like reserve airline and hotel tickets, order merchandise, manage your bank accounts, buy and sell stock, conduct information searches (scan current and back issues of newspapers and magazines, law libraries, medical journals, and so forth), check current news and weather forecasts, to name, truly, just a few. Collectively, these PC-based options are called on-line services. They are usually subscription- or fee-based. *See* page 41.

ON-SCREEN HELP. Operating assistance for applications that appear directly on the monitor, saving you the bother of looking them up in the manual. *See* page 68.

OPERATING ENVIRONMENT. One way of teaching children how to learn the piano is to put color strips over the keys. The idea is to make keys easier to identify and, consequently, to make the piano more familiar and accessible. Operating environments are a kind of software equivalent. They are usually intended to alter the look and feel of system software, making it more intuitive and accessible to users. This is particularly germane to DOS, an operating system many users find remote and impenetrable in its raw form. A number of operating environments have been developed for DOS, but the most prevalent by far is Microsoft Windows.

OPERATING SYSTEM. *See* SYSTEM SOFTWARE.

OPTICAL CHARACTER READER (OCR). A hardware peripheral that digitizes print, that is, converts it to software for storage or manipulation by word processors and other applications. *See* page 90.

OS. *See* SYSTEM SOFTWARE.

OS/2. An operating system created by Microsoft for high-end

ANTIDOTES
TO PC
ILLITERACY:
INDEX,
GLOSSARY,
AND
ENLIGHTENMENT
... IN PLAIN
ENGLISH

175

IBM PC-compatibles and most IBM PS machines. Although early forms of OS/2, pronounced "oh-ess-two," have been available for several years, most observers do not expect it to catch on widely until more OS/2 applications become available.

OUTPUT. Printed data, usually, in contrast to stored data.

PAGES PER MINUTE (PPM). *See* CHARACTERS PER SECOND.

PAINT PROGRAM. *See* FREEHAND PAINT AND DRAW PROGRAMS.

PARALLEL AND SERIAL COMMUNICATION. Information—instructions, data, and so forth—flows inside the PC and between the PC and hardware peripherals in two ways, all at once or in one chunk at a time. The all-at-once approach is called parallel communication; the one-chunk-at-a-time approach is called serial communication.

PARAMETER. A muddled and confusing word if there ever was one. Parameter seems to mean everything from *limits* to *condition* to *nature* as in "the parameters of the situation," depending on who's talking. Actually the word has a specialized mathematical definition, but if you need to know what it is, you can, as Casey Stengel was fond of saying, look it up. Most people and most hardware and software manuals use parameter to mean *option*, as in "Be sure to set your parameters before starting your work."

PC GURU. Anyone who knows more about personal computers than you do. Such people are to be flattered, cajoled, and laden with gifts. *See* page 149.

PERIPHERAL HARDWARE. *See* SYSTEM HARDWARE AND PERIPHERAL HARDWARE.

PERMANENT MEMORY. *See* LONG-TERM MEMORY.

PERSONAL INFORMATION MANAGER (PIM). Popular and usually inexpensive applications offering various combinations of familiar and not-so-familiar desktop accessories, typically including calendars, schedulers, address files, notepads, clocks (with alarms), spelling dictionaries, file-recovery utilities, and so forth. *See* page 31.

PIM. *See* PERSONAL INFORMATION MANAGER.

PIRATE. To make unauthorized copies of applications, which is to say, to steal.

PIXEL. A shortened form of *picture element.* The screen of a monitor is divided into rows and columns, forming hundreds of cells. Each cell is a single pixel. A pixel is the smallest unit on the screen that can be manipulated by programmers and users.

PLOTTER. *See* pages 61 and 100.

PLUG-IN BOARD. *See* ENHANCEMENT BOARD.

POINT AND CLICK. You operate some PCs by using an input device called a mouse to position an on-screen pointer over commands and pushing the mouse's execute button. This deliciously simple process has a simple straightforward name: point-and-click computing.

POINTER. *See* CURSOR/POINTER.

PERSONAL
COMPUTERS
FOR THE
COMPUTER
ILLITERATE

176

PORT. *See* PARALLEL AND SERIAL COMMUNICATION.

POWER USER. An experienced or technically savvy PC user or one who has mastered difficult, demanding applications.

PPM. *See* CHARACTERS PER SECOND.

PRACTICE MANAGEMENT. A category of business applications designed to help doctors, dentists, lawyers, accountants, consultants, contractors, free-lancers, and other independent professionals manage their practices. *See* page 46.

PREVENTIVE MAINTENANCE. As good an idea for PCs as for people. *See* page 147.

PRINTER. Most PC users agree that printers are the most important kind of peripheral hardware. You can start to inform yourself about printers—the choices and considerations—by turning to page 92.

PROCESSING SPEED. *See* page 112.

PRODUCT DEMONSTRATIONS. Just as you expect to test-drive a car before buying it, it's reasonable to expect to try out most kinds of hardware and software before purchasing them. *See* page 140.

PROGRAM. *See* APPLICATION PROGRAM.

PROGRAMMER. Someone who writes applications and other kinds of software containing coded instructions.

PROJECT MANAGEMENT. A PC application designed to help you manage projects by setting priorities, devising time lines, and so forth. *See* page 58.

PS/1 AND PS/2. *See* IBM PS SERIES.

PUBLIC DOMAIN SOFTWARE AND SHAREWARE. Public domain software is any application that has not been copyrighted and may be copied free of charge (usually without impinging on anyone's proprietary rights). Shareware refers to programs that have been copyrighted but may be purchased directly from the programmers who created them or from other suppliers for a nominal fee. Users are encouraged to pass on copies of shareware to other people, with the understanding that the new users will send payment to the programmer who created the shareware if they actually use the program.

PULLDOWN MENU. A list of commands that remains hidden from view until you "pull it down," usually by pointing and clicking with a computer mouse. *See* page 68.

QWERTY. The peculiar word, *qwerty*, comes from the order of the first six keys, reading left to right, on the top letter row of just about every typewriter and computer keyboard ever made. Look for yourself: Q-W-E-R-T-Y. Keyboards with this standard arrangement of letters and numerals are often called "qwerty keyboards."

The qwerty keyboard is interesting to many old hands in the personal computer industry because of what it reveals about the cursed durability of technological standards, even when those standards have outlived their usefulness.

You see, the greater efficiency of alternative keyboard arrangements has been demonstrated again and again over the years, but typists who have invested as much as a year to master qwerty have never been willing to abandon it simply because some time-and-motion expert could demonstrate a faster, more efficient keyboard layout. So ancient qwerty is still with us, an anachronism perhaps, but very much a standard, even on the slickest, fastest, most technologically advanced PCs on the market today.

RAM. *See* RANDOM ACCESS MEMORY.

RANDOM ACCESS MEMORY (RAM). Short-term memory, the hidden electronic work space inside the central processing unit in which all system software, programs, and data reside while they're active. When you call up an application from your hard disk or floppy, for example, your PC automatically places a copy of it in RAM, where it stays until you instruct the computer to remove it or until the power goes off. To preserve copies of your work, you have to "save" it in permanent memory—the hard disk or a floppy, a simple procedure (*see* SAVE). RAM is also called active memory and volatile memory. *See* pages 18, 80, 81, and 114.

READ. Your VCR *plays* a videotape, but your PC *reads* software.

READ-ONLY MEMORY (ROM). A phonograph record is significantly different from a tape in that you can play it—*read* it in PC lingo—but you cannot record on it. Therefore, you could say that records are a "play-only medium." Any PC medium that allows your machine to read programs stored on it but not to record on it is called read-only memory. Every PC comes with vital internal ROM programs stored within the CPU on ROM chips. These programs control the PC in ways that usually are not apparent to the user. They're like the deep brain in humans, regulating breathing and circulation beneath consciousness. Applications are also sometimes offered in ROM form.

REMOVABLE CARTRIDGE. A mass storage device. *See* page 83.

RENTING COMPUTER EQUIPMENT. Always an option.

REQUIREMENTS. You can't run just any old DOS application on any DOS PC or just any old Mac application on any Macintosh computer. Applications will only work if the PC meets minimum requirements. These vary from one application to another. *See* page 72.

REVOLUTIONARY. The single most popular and fantastical ("existing in the imagination; imaginary; unreal: as, the fantastic notions of the insane," to quote my old *Webster's*) advertising copy adjective in the PC industry. Savvy users train themselves to see through this word to the hype it usually represents.

ROM. *See* READ-ONLY MEMORY.

ROM DISK. *See* CD-ROM.

RS-232. An international communications standard employed in interfaces, cables, and connectors used in many personal computers.

SAVE. If you take a cassette tape recorder to a meeting and re-

ANTIDOTES
TO PC
ILLITERACY:
INDEX,
GLOSSARY,
AND
ENLIGHTENMENT
... IN PLAIN
ENGLISH

177

**PERSONAL
COMPUTERS
FOR THE
COMPUTER
ILLITERATE**

178

cord the proceedings, you capture them on tape. Fortunately, this is easy to do; you turn the machine on once and it generally continues to capture voices until it runs out of tape. Imagine a cassette recorder, however, that works by capturing sound temporarily. These temporary recordings are safe and can be played back only so long as you keep the machine turned on. If you turn the machine off, the recording is lost forever. To preserve your recording permanently, you have to press a "Preserve" button. But this only works retroactively; it preserves what's been recorded so far. Consequently you have to keep pushing the Preserve button to be sure of preserving ongoing proceedings. Believe it or not, this is how personal computers work. When you use an application to create data, write a letter, for example, the letter resides in short-term memory (RAM) until you do the PC-equivalent of pushing the Preserve button: enter a Save command, a blessedly quick and simple procedure on all PCs. Since "saving" only preserves work completed before, not after, you have to use it periodically, every few minutes, in fact, or you risk losing unpreserved data. That's why every PC adviser recommends that you

SAVE EARLY AND SAVE OFTEN

See page 154.

SCANNER.   A remarkable input device for digitizing (converting to software) printed text and images. *See* pages 50 and 90.

SERIAL COMMUNICATION.   *See* PARALLEL and SERIAL COMMUNICATION.

SHAREWARE.   *See* PUBLIC DOMAIN SOFTWARE AND SHAREWARE.

SIG.   *See* USER GROUP.

SILICON.   The main component of sand, the very stuff beaches are made of. Chemically speaking, silicon is a basic element like hydrogen, calcium, gold, and aluminum—an unfathomably abundant element comprising 28 percent of the earth's crust by weight. Most microchips are made of highly refined silicon.

SILICON VALLEY.   A broad flat valley at the southern end of San Francisco Bay once better known as the Santa Clara Valley, a more harmonious name for what was, not so long ago and not so far away, a far more harmonious and agricultural place. Silicon, nee Santa Clara, Valley is the home of Apple Computer, Hewlett-Packard, Intel, and many other computer-related companies.

SITE LICENSING.   One way to provide many users in one setting (a business, a corporate office, an institution) with access to multiple copies of a particular application. *See* page 143.

SLOT.   A space adjacent to the mother board (inside the central processing unit) reserved for enhancement boards, hardware components that enhance the performance of a personal computer. *See* page 80.

SOFTWARE.   You know what software is; you use it all the time, even if you don't have a personal computer. Videotapes are software (VCRs are hardware). Records and tapes and compact disks are software (record players and tape players and CD players are hardware). Film is software (cameras are hardware). In the personal computer universe, there are several kinds of common software, including applications, data, and systems software (operating systems). *See* page 9.

SPECIAL-INTEREST GROUP (SIG). *See* USER GROUP.

SPELLING CHECKER. A remarkable and remarkably useful application that everyone who uses a word processor, or plans to, should know about. *See* page 26.

SPREADSHEET. *See* ELECTRONIC SPREADSHEET.

STATIC ELECTRICITY. Potentially damaging to your computer and its disks, but if you're concerned, you can take precautions. *See* page 151.

STATISTICS SOFTWARE. *See* page 60.

SUPERCOMPUTER. The largest, costliest, and most powerful computers commercially available.

SUPPORT. A common verb and noun in PC-related advertising, product reviews, and the mouths of many commentators. As a verb it means "is compatible with" and as a noun, "compatibility." Consider the following sentence, for example. "QuasiStuf, which is very easy to install and use, supports most monitors and has good printer support." Translation: QuasiStuf is not only easy to install and use, it's compatible with most monitors and printers. Hardware and software companies that offer assistance to people who buy their products are said to offer "customer support."

SURGE PROTECTOR. A safeguard against spikes and surges in the power supply. *See* page 103.

SYSTEM BOARD. *See* MOTHER BOARD.

SYSTEM HARDWARE AND PERIPHERAL HARDWARE. There are basically two kinds of hardware: system and peripheral. System hardware is essential hardware, the minimal stuff you need to have a functional PC system. This includes the central processing unit, a monitor, disk drives, and input devices. Peripheral hardware is not vital for operating the system, but may be essential for some applications. Printers, modems, and scanners are examples of peripheral hardware. *See* pages 12, 78, and 92.

SYSTEM SOFTWARE. An essential master program, often called the operating system (OS), that runs the personal computer, manages applications, and provides services to the user. *See* page 9.

TAPE DRIVE. A mass storage device. *See* page 83.

TAX PLANNING AND PREPARATION SOFTWARE. *See* MONEY MANAGEMENT SOFTWARE.

TELECOMMUTING. Working at home, but staying in touch with clients, colleagues, and staff via electronic mail and other forms of PC communications. Telecommuting is getting more and more attention from the media, but remains exceptional.

TEMPLATE. A software template is usually a partially completed form that you customize by filling in the blanks according to

PERSONAL
COMPUTERS
FOR THE
COMPUTER
ILLITERATE

180

your needs. A keyboard template is a plastic crib sheet that lists frequently used commands and fits over the keyboard like a frame.

386 PC. *See* MICROPROCESSOR.

TOUCH SCREEN. A kind of input device. *See* page 89.

TRACK BALL. An input device best described as a stationary upside-down mouse. *See* page 88.

286 PC. *See* MICROPROCESSOR.

UNINTERRUPTIBLE POWER SUPPLY (UPS). A device that safeguards against sudden power dips or total power loss. *See* page 103.

UNIX AND XENIX. Unix is a kind of system software popular among scientists, engineers, and some academics. Relatively speaking, there aren't many commercial applications available for Unix, but some experts keep predicting that Unix will blossom in the wider PC community. Don't hold your breath. Xenix is Microsoft's version of Unix.

UPS. *See* UNINTERRUPTIBLE POWER SUPPLY.

USER. If you take bets for a living, work in a telephone exchange, or toil at a key punch machine you're an *operator*. If you haul customers around in a taxi, employ slave labor, or transport cattle overland, you're a *driver*. If you take advantage of people, indulge in drugs, or run a personal computer, you're a *user*.

USER GROUP. For every interest, hobby, syndrome, symptom, and cause, you can find a group of people who meet regularly to exchange information, plan events, support each other, and spread the faith. Why should personal computers be any different? Attending PC user groups can be a terrific way for newcomers to get questions answered. Many general user groups have subgroups called special-interest groups, or SIGs, usually including one devoted exclusively to the needs and problems of beginners. *See* page 134.

UTILITY. Usually a small, inexpensive program designed to enhance the performance of your personal computer or of particular applications. *See* page 64.

VDT. *See* MONITOR.

VERTICAL APPLICATIONS. Programs designed for specific professions or to do specialized kinds of work. Dentists can buy applications, for example, that are designed expressly to manage a dental practice scheduling, billing, ordering supplies, and so forth. There are hundreds of vertical applications available. Information about vertical applications is usually found in trade journals and association publications.

VIDEO DISPLAY TERMINAL (VDT). *See* MONITOR.

VIRUS. Any small, evil program designed to enter a computer without the user's knowledge. Some viruses are mere pranks, but others do terrible things like erase data permanently. Computer viruses are transmitted through phone lines when users hook up to electronic bulletin boards or through "infected" floppy disks. Many users guard against viruses by "inoculating" their computers with little programs designed to detect and destroy a virus before it can do any damage.

VOICE INPUT. Executing commands and entering data by talking to the computer rather than by manipulating conventional input devices. *See* page 91.

WARRANTIES. Hardware and software warranties are like the warranties for most consumer products: They're limited and have lots of small print. Still, they offer important protection. *See* page 140.

WHAT YOU SEE IS WHAT YOU GET. *See* WYSIWYG.

WINDOW. Some VCRs allow you to show one channel in a small inset box while watching another channel, full-sized, on the regular TV screen. In PCs, such boxes are called windows. They allow you to display several activities on the monitor simultaneously.

WINDOWS. *See* MICROSOFT WINDOWS.

WORD PROCESSOR. One of the traditional "Big Three" PC applications (along with database management systems and electronic spreadsheets). If a PC user has only one application, more likely than not it's a word processor. Word processors are a good deal more than PC versions of typewriters. *See* page 21.

WORKSTATION. A souped-up PC or a kind of minicomputer, depending on who's defining it. Whichever, workstations are powerful, specialized, and expensive desktop computers used mainly by scientists, engineers, and other technically inclined professionals. *See* page 129.

WYSIWYG. Pronounced wizzy-wig, an acronym for What You See Is What You Get. Translation: What you see on the screen is exactly what you get on paper when you print. This is a very desirable, but far from universal, quality in PC applications. *See* page 69.

XENIX. *See* UNIX AND XENIX.

Ø. The numeral zero. The slash is used to distinguish it from a capital *O*, the first letter of Owen.

ANTIDOTES
TO PC
ILLITERACY:
INDEX,
GLOSSARY,
AND
ENLIGHTENMENT
... IN PLAIN
ENGLISH

181

ABOUT THE AUTHOR

BARRY OWEN is a magazine management consultant and coauthor of *Waldenbooks Computer NewsLink*, a quarterly newsletter. His education with PCs began when he was a self-described computer illiterate serving as managing editor of *PC Magazine* where he went on to become executive editor. He was intimately involved with the launching of *PC Week*, *A+*, *Digital Review*, *PC Disk Magazine*, *PC Product Guide*, and *Computer Industry Daily*. He also helped launch *Microsoft Systems Journal* and *PC Computing*, and has been involved with *MacUser*, *PC Tech Journal*, and *PC World* magazine.